About the Series

The purpose of this series of books is to provide an international exchange of ideas and to explore different approaches in professional therapy practice. The books are written primarily for experienced clinicians. They are not intended as basic texts nor as reports on the most recent research, though elements of these aspects may be included.

Articles written by experts from a number of different countries form the core of each volume. These are supported by a commentary on the current 'state of the art' in the particular area of practice and an annotated bibliography of key references.

Each volume covers a topic which we believe to be of universal interest. Some are concerned with a troublesome symptom (for example Volume 1 on Pain edited by T. Hoskins Michel); others are related to problems within a broad diagnostic category, for example this volume.

I. B.
N. T. W.

VOLUME EDITORS

Mette Sveram

Mette Sveram has been the principal at the College of Physiotherapy in Oslo since 1974. She has been in charge of physiotherapy at Sunnaas Hospital, a rehabilitation centre, for many years, and has also worked as a physiotherapist in general hospitals and in private practice. In 1973 she attended the Sargent College of Allied Health Professions at Boston University on a special student programme. She is a former president of the Norwegian Physiotherapy Association (1968–1972) and was a member of the board for several years. Mette Sveram has been a member/chairman on a wide variety of committees appointed by the Norwegian State, volunteer organizations and the Norwegian Physiotherapy Association. The committees deal with matters of health care, physiotherapy, education and research. She is President of the Norwegian Physiotherapy Association Committee on Ethics.

Tove Hegna

Tove Hegna is an Executive Officer in Oslo Central Administration, Division of Decentralized Health and Social Services. Until recently she was Director of Physiotherapy in the Oslo City Health Department (Oslo Helseråd) and on the staff of the Commissioner of Health in Oslo. Her experience has been varied, her main interest and clinical experience being in physiotherapy for psychosomatic conditions. She attended Boston University's Special International Student Programme in 1968/1969 and was for 12 years a teacher at the College of Physiotherapy in Oslo. She has been a member of the editorial board of the Norwegian Physiotherapy Journal and served on several committees dealing with educational planning as well as health administration. She was president of the Norwegian Physiotherapy Association in 1982 when the Norwegian Municipal Health Act was adopted which caused physiotherapy to become a mandatory service in the municipalities. As a result her term of office became a period of intensive planning and development for a new community physiotherapy service in Norway. From 1983, as a Director of the Physiotherapy Department in Oslo Helseråd, she aimed at establishing physiotherapy as an integrated service in primary health care in Oslo, along with home nursing, health centres and kindergartens. In this way she helped to provide a rehabilitation service for the chronically ill and handicapped who are not institutionalized but live in their own homes.

INTERNATIONAL PERSPECTIVES IN PHYSICAL THERAPY 5

Psychological and Psychosomatic Problems

Edited by

Tove Hegna RPT CertSpecStudy
Executive Officer, Oslo Central Administration, Division of Decentralized Health
and Social Services, Oslo, Norway

Mette Sveram RPT CertSpecStudy
Director of the College of Physiotherapy,
Oslo, Norway

Foreword by
Nancy Theilgaard Watts RPT PhD
Professor in the Physical Therapy Graduate Program, MGH Institute of Health
Professions, Massachusetts General Hospital, Boston, USA

CHURCHILL LIVINGSTONE
EDINBURGH LONDON MELBOURNE AND NEW YORK 1990

CHURCHILL LIVINGSTONE
Medical Division of Longman Group UK Limited

Distributed in the United States of America by Churchill
Livingstone Inc., 1560 Broadway, New York, N.Y. 10036,
and by associated companies, branches and representatives
throughout the world.

First published 1990

ISBN 0-443-03347-1
ISSN 0267–0380

British Library Cataloguing in Publication Data
Psychological and psychosomatic problems.
  1. Man. Psychosomatic diseases. Therapy
  I. Hegna, Tove   II. Sveram, Mette   III. Series
  616.08

Library of Congress Cataloging in Publication Data
Psychological and psychosomatic problems/[edited by] Tove Hegna, Mette
  Sveram.
      p. cm. — (International perspectives in physical therapy,
  ISSN 0267–0380 : 5)
      Bibliography: p.
      Includes index.
      ISBN 0-443-03347-1
      1. Physical therapy — Psychological aspects.   2. Medicine,
  Psychosomatic.   I. Hegna, Tove.   II. Sveram, Mette.   III. Series [DNLM:
  1. Physical Therapy.   2. Psychophysiologic Disorders — therapy.   W1
  IN827JM v. 5 / WM 405 P974]
  RM701.P73   1989
  615.8'2'019–dc20
  DNLM/DLC
  for Library of Congress   89-9793
                                                                          CIP

Produced by Longman Singapore Publishers (Pte) Ltd.
Printed in Singapore

Foreword

This volume is a particularly welcome addition to the *International Perspectives in Physical Therapy* series. It clearly demonstrates the value of an exchange of ideas among therapists from different countries; and, for many therapists, it will open a door on a relatively unexplored area of clinical practice.

Although several of the approaches described in this book have been known for years to many therapists in Scandinavia, information about them has not been readily accessible to therapists in other countries. The collection of papers assembled by Mette Sveram and Tove Hegna offers readers an unparalleled opportunity to learn about and to compare a variety of different approaches to evaluation and treatment of psychological and psychosomatic problems. Equally important, these papers provide a valuable step towards development of sound clinical theory in an area of clinical practice that has lacked systematic guidelines in the past.

Many of the basic ideas espoused by the contributors to this book will seem familiar to most therapists. Early in their training physical therapy students are told they must be sensitive, understanding and humane, as well as technically competent. Most graduate therapists would agree with the general belief that interdependence of mind and body cannot be ignored, and that good treatment must reflect an intelligent concern for both domains. As they touch and observe their patients, therapists soon discover that the non-verbal messages of the body may be more useful and revealing than the things patients put into words. Despite this, the efforts of many therapists to interpret and respond to psychological factors often are haphazard and half-hearted. Translating general beliefs and vague concepts into practical action is difficult without a logical framework for reasoning. To date the physical therapy profession has developed few systematic methods for evaluating the individual patient's psychological assets and liabilities, lacks a common language for describing observations and interventions in this arena, and has little organized theory to guide the therapist's response to psychological components of the problems treated. The papers in this book take a giant step towards overcoming these deficiences. Some draw on the research literature in psychology to point out findings of potential importance for physical therapy and suggest practical ways in which they might be applied. Others draw on the rich experience of observant clinicians and describe the approaches to patient evaluation and treatment they have developed through years of thoughtful work with patients.

The papers in this book should both stimulate and guide future work to develop physical therapy practice in the area of psychological and psychosomatic disorders. Although few of them report objective data on the results achieved, the theories and methods described represent useful and thought-provoking clinical hypotheses about holistic practice in physical therapy. However, few of these hypotheses have been thoroughly and impartially tested. This then is the challenge to the reader. The full value of this book cannot be realized if its readers become interested only in learning more practical detail about the approaches outlined briefly in these pages. Interest in learning how to use these methods should be accompanied by a strong commitment to related clinical research. Designing sound studies to determine the effects of these treatments will not be an easy job. The effects of greatest importance are often complex and not readily measured using the quantitative, physical measures with which physical therapists are most familiar. Continued exploration of qualitative research methods and of the designs used by investigators in the social sciences will be needed. These efforts can both help us move towards fuller understanding of the psychological components of clinical practice and let us validate, refine and extend the important work done by the contributors to this book.

N.T.W

Contributors

Inge Bloch RPT
Physiotherapist, International Rehabilitation and Research Centre for Torture Victims (RCT), Copenhagen, Denmark

Berit Heir Bunkan RPT MagArt
Senior Lecturer, College of Physiotherapy, Oslo, Norway

Therese Cimini RPT PhD
Co-Director, Boston Neurobehavioral Center, Boston, USA

Karin Denstad RPT
Physical Therapist, Health Services at the University of Oslo, Norway

Tove Hegna RPT CertSpecStudy
Executive Officer, Oslo Central Administration, Division of Decentralized Health and Social Services, Oslo, Norway

Lillemor Johnsen
Psychotherapist and physiotherapist. Holder of permanent state scholarship, private practitioner, Oslo, Norway

Grete Møller RPT
Physiotherapist, International Rehabilitation and Research Centre for Torture Victims (RCT), Copenhagen, Denmark

Cecily Partridge BA (Hons) PhD FCSP
Director, Centre for Physiotherapy Research, King's College London, UK

Gjertrud Roxendal RPT DMSc
Department of Physical Therapy, Lund University, Sweden

Mette Sveram RPT CertSpecStudy
Director of the College of Physiotherapy, Oslo, Norway

Eline Thornquist RPT
Research Scholar at the University of Oslo, Norway

There are no absolutes for something so relative as a human life.

From Prather Hugh 1970 Notes to Myself. Real People Press, Utah

My growth does not seem to be a matter of learning new lessons, but of learning the old lessons again and again. The wisdom doesn't change, only the situations.

In order to break with a habit I will first have to become aware of how I **usually** *act. I will have to see how I do it before I can undo it. At the time, I am not aware of how I shut down my attention or hold back my warmth.*

Allowing the pain to talk to me. **Listening** *to the complaints of my body. Noticing what my ulcer forces me to do.*

I am beginning to see that most of my illnesses have been an externalization of an internal conflict, that my body gets sick whenever I am not letting go.

How do I keep people out? What am I doing with my words, my eyes, to hold this person away? Am I letting his voice touch me, or am I only hearing it? Am I using my eyes to see him or to 'look him in the eye'?

How much tension have I pressed into my body, how much have I strained to keep myself under control? Is it any wonder that I am stiff after compressing myself inside a vice for thirty-three years?

I see that tensing my butt and taking shallow breaths go together. It is difficult for me to take a full abdominal breath and still maintain a tight butt. Now I want to see what will happen if I start breathing fully the next time I notice that I am holding myself back emotionally.

This evening I finally did it: I stopped giving myself a headache. When I felt it coming on I stood very still, and let go of all the pushing — and for the rest of the evening my neck and head felt free.

There were seventy-five people in the lobby and only a seven-year-old girl was finding out what it felt like to sit on a marble floor.

'Growth' can get to be such a deadly business.

Contents

Section Two

SECTION ONE

1. Introduction

T. Hegna & M. Sveram

This book discusses the use of physiotherapy in some groups of patients with psychosomatic and psychological problems.

The relationship between psyche and soma has been the focus of intense research during the last few decades. This has resulted in a sounder scientific basis for an understanding of the holistic approach.

A psychosomatic holistic approach involves the understanding that most, if not all, of the body's healthy and diseased functions are influenced by and influence psychic functions (Mellgren et al, 1983). This insight has been scientifically proved. The influences are sometimes clear-cut but are most often difficult to determine. This is the case, for example, in the healing of wounds and development of antibodies in the body's immune system. The relationship is more obvious in the large group of patients who seek help through physiotherapy for, for example, nervous tension conditions and various musculoskeletal disorders.

In recent literature, we find a wide acceptance of the idea that sickness and health are the result of a mutual interaction and influence of psychological, physical and social factors in a person's life, and that these factors must all be taken into consideration.

To take such claims and acknowledgements seriously will necessarily lead to major changes in patient treatment. Are we willing to accept the challenge?

The articles in this book show examples of physiotherapy aimed mainly at patients with more or less clearly defined psychological problems, e.g. stress and tension in the musculoskeletal system. The treatment approaches have similarities but are different in methodology, areas of indication, and in their practical application. Several of the methods have been developed by physiotherapists who, over a period of time, have tried and tested them, gathered new information and constantly acquired new experience through

3

practice. These methods have been developed through work with patients rather than through scientific testing. This should not stop us from taking the methods seriously, however. Many of today's methods of medical treatment have in fact grown out of long experience acquired by good clinicians. It is perhaps not until later that certain elements of the methodology can be supported scientifically. The dynamics of human relationships, which are an important part of physiotherapy and of the therapeutic process, cannot be measured by the traditional scientific objective methods which medical science in the West has for the most part relied upon.

If we are to extend the boundaries of physiotherapy, we must have the courage to accept the experience of colleagues with long systematic practice. Combined with sound criticism and gradual substantiation through new knowledge and experimentation, this must provide us with as justifiable a foundation in physiotherapy as in medicine in general. Several of the authors emphasize the qualitative aspects in their methods of examination and treatment. It is important to take these aspects into account even though they may be difficult to prove scientifically.

The personality and experience of the physiotherapist are important, as well as her skills and techniques, in the treatment of patients.

In the interaction between therapist and patient, the therapist's personal resources are brought into use. She communicates not only through her hands, but also through her behaviour and general way of being, through her particular expressions of feeling.

Important opportunities in therapy are lost if the therapist is not conscious of this and does not have the courage to develop and use her personal insight, feelings, and experience in patient treatment. This represents a therapeutic challenge that could create a new dimension in physiotherapy practice if we dare to take it.

Many physiotherapists are reluctant to cross what they see as traditional professional boundaries, and they find it difficult to see where the dividing line lies between physiotherapy and psychology/psychotherapy. It is important to note that all the authors in this book take *the body* as the point of departure for understanding the patient's problems. This is precisely where the physiotherapist's strength lies and it is here that our profession has a distinct potential which is different from most other health professions. From this starting point a therapeutic process can be developed. How far the process goes is dependent on the individual physiotherapist's knowledge, level of personal maturity, and experience.

A holistic approach involves an understanding of the patient's environment and social situation as well. These are factors that will play a part in the therapeutic process and in determining how much the patient will benefit from physiotherapy.

THE GENERAL HEALTH OF THE POPULATION

Several of the authors in this book point out the necessity for a more holistic approach as a basis for understanding and influencing people's health. Because of this we have found it natural to place the theme of the book in a wider perspective. We will therefore describe briefly some important aspects of health in the West, including the extent of psychosomatic, psychological and psychiatric disorders. We will also discuss certain consequences which the scientific philosophy of the West has had on our view of health and disease, and look at the importance of physiotherapy in this context.

A prevalent view is that people's health has declined in the West during the last 20—30 years. This is reflected in, for example, the increase in alcohol, narcotic and tobacco abuse. We see problems of co-existence, divorces, lonely people and a large number of unemployed people. We also see this decline reflected in the increasing numbers of people seeking out health services for relief from what we call life-style diseases.

In Norway, for example, the most common complaints of those seeking primary health services are musculoskeletal and psychological disorders. An increase in the number of health service visits as well as in the use of medicines has also been reported, and a larger part of the population in general feels ill. Similar results and tendencies are also found in other countries in the West. This development is a serious problem for those involved in forming health policy, as well as for those working in the health services, especially since modern Western society has invested extensive financial and human resources in finding ways to improve the population's health.

Yet at the same time medicine has made remarkable progress that just a few years ago would have been thought impossible. Superior forms of treatment have been developed for a number of serious illnesses such as cancer and cardiovascular diseases; advanced medical technology has led to better and safer conditions for surgery.

Many other examples could be mentioned. It is therefore important, especially in the light of increased criticism of the health system, that we do not lose sight of the positive aspects of today's health services.

In this context it is of central importance that health personnel in particular realize that not all health problems can or should be solved by the health professions. Many of the problems presented to the health sector can be said to be symptoms of more deeply-rooted problems of society. If the health system continues uncritically to treat the symptoms of society's social and economic difficulties as if they had a medical cause, we may risk an even greater increase in health problems.

Studies have been made of the various factors that influence health. Some studies show that the health services have a limited effect on people's health. It is said that only 10% of all health problems can be solved within the health sector. The remaining 90% must be solved through self-care and through socio-political measures (Hjort, 1982).

The World Health Organization refers to a possible health crisis by the year 2000 'unless radical steps are taken by the public, the professions, industry and the European countries as well as USA, to change the situation' (O'Neill, 1983).

It is also interesting to note the increasing tendency of people with complaints and ailments who do not get the help they need through the traditional health services to seek out alternative forms of treatment. In Denmark approximately 25–50% of the population seek out such alternative medicine (Risom Petersen, 1986). This must be seen as an indirect criticism of traditional medicine as well as an indication that today's health services are inadequate. This, however, seldom leads to serious debate among health professions so the status quo is maintained.

That the present health care service has little effect on the general health of the population can to some extent be blamed on the fact that treatments given cannot solve problems that have complex and composite causes.

In summary, we can say that despite large investments and positive results within the health services in most Western countries, the general state of health has not improved as would be expected.

EXTENT OF PSYCHOLOGICAL DISEASES

Statistically there are approximately 40 million people with mental/psychological diseases in the world today. In Europe over one million people with such diseases are still in mental hospitals (O'Neill, 1983).

Prolonged psychological diseases are most often found in people over 50, but there is also an increase in younger age groups. Nearly twice as many women as men have long-standing psychological ailments. Other high risk groups are divorced people and people with low education or low social status (Helsedirektoratet, 1987).

A high degree of mental illness is also reported among the elderly. In England, for example, a quarter of all patients committed to psychiatric institutions are over 65. These individuals suffer mainly from depression and anxiety — in other words senile dementia is not the only or even the greatest problem in this group. One study also shows that individuals over 65 who take their own life represent one third of all suicides in England each year (Hare, 1986). In the USA studies show that up to 25% of the American population suffer from psychological problems.

These figures tell us something about the number of people who are diagnosed as having mental/psychological diseases, even though there is a large degree of uncertainty attached to the figures. Whether a disease is registered as mental/psychological often depends on medical and diagnostic tradition. It will also depend on the development of and access to health services in various countries. Cultural traditions as well as views on illness and health will play an important role. Lack of agreement in judgement and tradition means that the extent of psychosomatic ailments is impossible to quantify, and probably, in fact, uninteresting.

THE EFFECTS OF THE SCIENTIFIC PHILOSOPHY OF THE WEST ON THE UNDERSTANDING OF HEALTH AND DISEASE

'The progress in the Western world has occurred predominately in the areas of the rational and the intellectual. To a greater extent than in any other culture or civilisation in history, we have lost contact with our biological and ecological foundation. We see a striking cleft between the development of intellectual capacities, scientific insight and technical possibilities on the one hand — and wisdom, spirituality and ethics on the other.' (Capra, 1986)

We have to go far back in history to find the roots of modern medicine. If we go as far back as Hippocrates (460–377 BC) we will see that in medicine he integrated two important aspects: that a human being undergoes a constant process of change with in-built capacities for healing; while at the same time he must heed natural laws in order to maintain a balance.

This holistic view of human beings disappeared after Hippocrates and the approach to medical science in the West has changed from a holistic-biological viewpoint to a mechanical-physical one.

The philosopher and mathematician Rene Descartes (1595–1650) played an important part in this development. He was at that time the first to distinguish between the consciousness and the body and propounded the view that all living organisms can be understood mechanically. Descartes himself believed in the connection between these two parts, but as a result of his philosophy the medical profession concentrated on the body (Capra 1986). This has played a major role in the development of science, and medical science. With his analytic approach, which involved breaking down thoughts and problems into small units and deducing a logical structure for their composition, Descartes has had a decisive influence on scientists in the West, whether they be biologists, psychologists or medical doctors.

After bacteria were discovered approximately 100 years ago, medical science has been influenced by the natural science approach, with illness being principally explained by physical and chemical laws.

One consequence of this has been that medical science has mainly concentrated on conditions of illness in the human being. Positive personal resources and the individual's own potential for development have been given less emphasis. As a result, insight into cause and effect between health and life situation has been underrated in the health sector and in society.

Another consequence has been that when an individual learns that an illness has been brought on by bacteria found outside the body, it is easy for him to believe that he is merely a passive victim of outside forces of nature. He may also believe that his own feelings have nothing to do with illness and that he has little control over his own health.

Another important element that served to strengthen this belief was the Church. There has been, right up to the present day, a widespread belief that illness was God's punishment for a life of sin. It was therefore either God or the doctor who was responsible for recovery. How a person lived was hardly important for his health.

The dualism that developed between the spiritual individual and the physical individual helped to cure many diseases, but it created problems as well.

Looking back one can say that the chief characteristic of scientific thinking during the past 250−300 years has been a remarkable simplification. The world has been divided in two — one part is physical and can be weighed and measured purely scientifically; while the other, the spiritual world, is non-material and composed of spirit, feelings and thoughts that are hard to measure: this second part has been left to religion and philosophy far into our century.

This distinction between an individual's body and his soul has also characterized treatment and research within the fields of psychiatry and psychology.

However, with Sigmund Freud came the development of a new view of the human psyche: the discovery of the unconscious and its dynamics. His theory is known as dynamic psychiatry and focusses on the forces that create psychological disturbances. He attaches great importance to childhood experiences and their consequences for an individual's later development.

One of Freud's pupils, Wilhelm Reich, has played a major role in our understanding of psychological factors and emotional experience and how these phenomena can create resistance in the body in the form of muscular tension. One of his most important discoveries was that attitudes and emotional experiences cause certain tension patterns in the muscles that block a free energy flow. His discovery has had consequences for physiotherapists working with psychosomatic problems and in psychiatry.

In today's society there is a general belief that health and illness are extremes on a one-dimensional scale despite the fact that most people realize that the relationship is not so simple. A physical illness can be offset by a positive attitude and by social support so that the result is a general sense of well-being. Likewise emotional problems or social isolation can make a person feel ill, or become ill, despite good physical health.

Medical science in the modern Western world has based its skills on scientific research. The focus is on the diseased organism, i.e. that which is dysfunctional in the living organism, the pathological changes in cells and tissues.

This view reduces the human being to a physical body and stands in sharp contrast to the view that the human organism is a living system in which all parts/elements are intrinsically related to and dependent on each other and — ideally — of equal importance. Health is thus defined as a condition of total balance and illness as a sign that an organism has lost this balance. Illness is, in this ideology, a positive signal that should lead to an initiative to restore health by analysing and eliminating the possible cause(s) (Risom Petersen, 1986).

Our conception and understanding of health and illness are, in other words, decisive in determining how an individual's illness and suffering will be treated, since 'health' has many dimensions that each play a part in the complex interplay between the physical, psychological and social aspects of a human being.

WHERE DOES PHYSIOTHERAPY STAND?

As editors of this book we have found it difficult to get physio-therapists to write about the psychological aspects of somatic and preventative physiotherapy to the extent we had hoped. We see this as an indication that we as a professional group fail, in written form, to communicate the significance of the emotional and environmental aspects of disease. In looking through books, articles, reports, recommendations, etc., while preparing this book, it is remarkable and disappointing how infrequently physio-therapists are mentioned or have themselves produced inde-pendent contributions.

Most physiotherapists would agree that their treatment/practice of physiotherapy is based on an understanding of the close connection between an individual's body, psyche and environ-ment.

Physiotherapists have, however, like many others in the health sector, begun to ask whether we are as holistic in our practice as we believe ourselves to be. Many claim that we as a profession are influenced by scientifically-oriented Western medicine more than we care to admit, with all the limitations this has for our professional practice.

The debates within physiotherapy in Scandinavian countries

have made clear the dualism existing in physiotherapy as well as in Western medicine and in Western culture in general. Many have been preoccupied with and written about this dualism.

We can say that there are two points of view that have characterized physiotherapy in recent years. R. Piene (1979), physiotherapist and sociologist, says that the goal for physiotherapists is to establish causality. It becomes a primary task to further develop the diagnostic apparatus and to make as exact a function-analysis as possible. To take objective measurements and quantify the results of treatment should be a goal for successful treatment. Further, she claims that this requirement has to a large extent come from physiotherapists themselves, and has been closely connected to the desire to develop a profession that functions independently of medicine. It is also important, we may add, that physiotherapists in this way also gain respect and acceptance among doctors.

On the other hand, she says that the basis for all treatment is the acknowledgement that symptoms and reduced function in the musculoskeletal system can often be a manifestation of complex processes for which it would be difficult or impossible to identify a simple cause. The focus here is on the interplay between several factors. In this perspective the symptom's communicative aspect is emphasized. With this mode of thinking, the physiotherapist may wonder whether physiotherapy in fact represents an adequate solution to the patient's particular problem, even though he/she presents with a physical symptom. The main task would be to bring the patient into a dialectic process that aims to discover a relationship between the symptom and the patient's physical, psychological and social situation.

It is our belief that physiotherapists who work with people whose psychological problems are primary or acknowledged as contributing factors in somatic illness appear to have a greater awareness and understanding of the relationship between the physical, psychological and social factors in an individual than physiotherapists who work with patients whose somatic illness is the main symptom.

If physiotherapists are to adopt a holistic approach they must develop a new attitude to the patient's psychosocial situation, acknowledging especially the significance of emotions in the treatment process.

A more holistic approach will also affect policy on the prevention of disease, treatment, research and training of physiotherapists. The research or scientific methods we choose will, for example, determine the kind of training that takes place in our schools as well as in our practice. Purely quantitative research is incapable of taking into account experiences, qualities and values.

Gunn Engelsrud points out that it is important to find out how physiotherapists can do research to describe experiences obtained from physiotherapy practice without using scientific methods which involve a separation between the subject and the object, between body and soul etc. This means that we will have to develop and systematize what happens *in the process* of physiotherapy. We must develop methods which consider that subject and object are in a continuous relationship and therefore in mutual understanding. A body awareness where the different parts of the body are understood, regarded and treated in isolation without an understanding of the interplay within the body, the breath in the body and the body and its surroundings in totality, will have obvious weaknesses.

An alternative understanding is therefore necessary to state the reasons for practice. Within psychology and medicine the splitting of body/soul is an unsolved problem. Both the body and the psyche are looked upon as limited and distinct. Because psychodynamic and medical understanding so strongly dominate physiotherapy, it is difficult to find words for an alternative understanding.

If physiotherapy, however, continues to be based upon a dualistic comprehension of the body, it is possible that we as a profession will orient ourselves away from the body as it exists, and develop physiotherapy within either a psycho/social or a physical/mechanical framework.

Neither of these forms will, according to Gunn Engelsrud, be able to catch or logically explain the reality of the living and active body, and consequently will generate dualism.

Most chapters in this book describe problems and approaches/methods in physiotherapy that apply to individuals with psychiatric illness or psychosomatic complaints. It has been difficult to find physiotherapists who would write about the psychological aspects of patients with major injuries and various handicaps, for example in elderly people. Partridge refers to these areas in her chapter without mentioning particular groups, such as patients with burn injuries, amputations, spinal injuries, stroke, etc.

In the following paragraphs we will emphasize elements in the various chapters that we feel are of special interest, both for physiotherapy in general and where psychological factors play a central role in physiotherapy treatment.

Bloch and Møller's chapter on torture gives perhaps the clearest expression of how important it is to take into consideration the relationship between the psyche, soma and social conditions. Experience from work with torture victims shows that treatment will not be successful unless all of these factors are considered. Psychological and physical afflictions may perhaps improve, but the best results are obtained when social aspects, such as contact with the family and culture, are taken into account. The type of physiotherapy that is practised with these patients is neither remarkable nor considerably different from so-called ordinary physiotherapy. However, there must exist a cross-professional cooperation with shared responsibility and empathy. It is necessary to understand that the tortured person's self-image may be totally changed, and this requires a great deal of sensitivity on the part of those in the team including the physiotherapist.

Cimini describes how many of the traumas and symptoms that torture victims experience are the same as those that victims of abuse, rape and major injuries may experience. Self-confidence, which is fundamental for man's existence, may be disturbed or destroyed.

Besides requiring empathy, sensitivity and understanding, the treatment of these problems makes demands on the physio-therapist's personal development and requires insight into the psychological aspects of treatment.

Cimini also points out the importance of becoming aware of the difference between traumas that create psychological problems and traumas that result in the same problems but that are of a neurophysiological nature.

Partridge in her chapter discusses in detail the psychological factors involved in treating patients with physical disabilities. She emphasizes the necessity of increased knowledge and awareness of these factors in understanding and improving communication between the therapist and the patient/client, particularly to improve rehabilitation results. This is especially important in the treatment of individuals with permanent and major physical handicaps. Motivation and levels of aspiration, for example, are closely connected. If the physiotherapist is more concerned with specific muscles and movements while the patient is more interested in how he/she will be able to function in the home, there will be poor interaction and the patient's motivation will be reduced.

Agreeing on a common goal — or coming to some form of mutual agreement — will contribute to an increased motivation and create a realistic basis for expectations. Several authors emphasize the necessity of such an agreement. Patients must to a greater extent contribute to decision-making and help set up guidelines for their goals and treatment.

Denstad says in her chapter that a necessary condition for successful treatment is that a contract or agreement is worked out between patient and therapist. This assumes that the physiotherapist enters into dialogue with the patient where the patient's motivation and goals are discussed and made clear, and an agreement is reached as to how the goals are to be attained.

Denstad describes in her article Autogenic Training (AT) one of many relaxation techniques. AT is similar to meditation in that it is based on ideas and thoughts from Eastern medicine. Treatment may be given individually, but is first of all given in groups. The treatment must be seen as a preventive measure for more healthy individuals suffering from stress and diffuse myalgic pains. Denstad accepts the patients' more concrete complaints, yet in contrast to what is otherwise common practice in physiotherapy, the symptoms are not focussed upon. The author asks the question to what extent this relaxation method is physiotherapy, but has no difficulties in answering the question herself.

The method Denstad describes brings the physiotherapist face to face with new therapeutic challenges. It involves new ways of working and requires that the physiotherapist work actively on self-development. Body awareness, body language and feelings, and her own attitudes, are areas the therapist must be willing to work on.

Several of the authors are of the opinion that traditional physiotherapy — which is not defined — is not adequate in solving the problems which are the main reason that many patients/clients seek physiotherapy. This can only be understood to mean that physiotherapists often speak and theorize about holistic approaches, but they seldom actually practise such approaches. Partridge emphasizes this explicitly.

Bunkan & Thornquist discuss this problem in their chapter. They emphasize that the body is a functioning and interacting entity in which the psyche and the soma are inseparable — an individual is always mind and body at the same time. The body is seen as a dynamic phenomenon; respiration is seen as a barometer; and the relationship between muscular tension and respiration are considered central if one aims at a holistic understanding of human beings. They point out how unfortunate the dualistic view in medicine (as well as in physiotherapy) in the Western world has been for our way of treating patients. As an example, they mention how physiotherapists are taught to see respiration from a pathological point of view, and not from the point of view and understanding of the role breathing plays in regulating feelings, or in the role feelings play in regulating breathing.

The authors go on to say that psychomotor treatment and therapy are built on those aspects just mentioned. Much of this has had consequences for the Norwegian practice of physiotherapy. For example, it is no longer common to correct physical body posture. The reason for this is that a person's posture is an expression of his character and personality. Experience from psychomotor treatment tells us that body posture changes automatically when muscle tension balance is improved and respiration is freed.

As in Denstad's chapter, pain and tension are taken as indications that some aspect of that individual's life is not functioning as it should. The focus is therefore not on the symptom, but on bodily and emotional reactions. It is necessary to try to make the patient/client aware of this interaction. Helping a patient/client to see and experience the relationship between symptoms and life-situation becomes an important part of the treatment.

Roxendal in her chapter deals principally with physiotherapy in psychiatric hospitals. She works for the most part with groups of patients and emphasizes body awareness in its wider meaning. Psychiatric care is undergoing great changes which are found in many areas of Western health care services, and they reflect the fact that an increasing number of people are realizing that our traditional ways of organizing health services do not result in improved health, and they are uneconomical as well. Investing in primary health services with greater emphasis on rehabilitation and open care, and with wider cross-professional cooperation, characterizes this development in the health service.

Roxendal points out that the physiotherapist must develop a greater awareness of the use of her own time and of others' time.

The question of priority is discussed: which patients; how often; what a patient himself, relatives and family, and other health personnel, can do if given guidance and instruction from the physiotherapist; and what the physiotherapist has to do herself.

These problems are perhaps most pressing in psychiatry where the physiotherapist's resources have been limited and the number of patients large. Those physiotherapists who in recent years have worked with psychiatric patients have therefore developed less traditional ways of working.

Roxendal raises the question of how results should be measured, and several of the other authors also bring this up in their chapters. This is one of the greatest challenges to physiotherapy, because it will become important to make use of scientific methods other than those used in natural science which have so far influenced medicine and physiotherapy.

Roxendal also discusses how important it is that a physiotherapist continues to develop herself as a person. In this context the development of the therapist's personality is more important than methods and techniques. It is interesting that many physiotherapists in Sweden have sought out various therapy forms for their own development; several of them have chosen a Chinese method that is based on an integrated holistic view.

The chapter that will perhaps be the most controversial is the chapter written by Johnsen. Her theory and therapy have been developed through experience in treating people with serious psychological problems. She uses certain expressions commonly used in medicine, but with new meanings, and she gives her own definitions of these concepts. Fundamental to her theory is the belief that the most essential element in a human being is happiness and that a healthy individual, whose whole body breathes, is able to develop and find the means to continue on, unimpeded, through the various stages of his development.

The theory and treatment may appear difficult to understand, perhaps for the most part because we are all products of the Western world's fragmented and dualistic way of looking at human beings.

What is distinctive about Johnsen's theory, IRT (Integrated Respiratory Theory), is that it is not the musculature itself that is most important, but rather the 'breathing'. Respiration is the most essential element, along with the therapist's ability to use IRT to find out where respiration is blocked.

The quality of the musculature will reflect the emotional conflicts in the body. The goal is to bring out hidden feelings and resources so that experiences and feelings can be worked through.

W. Reich describes how attitudes and feelings can get stuck in muscles and block a free energy flow. Of major importance for Reich was therefore to loosen up the tight hypertonic musculature since there cannot be spontaneous activity before the muscular tension is reduced. This view has influenced physiotherapy.

According to Johnsen, it is her experience that it is towards the hypotonic muscular condition that treatment should be directed. Underdeveloped musculature indicates on the one hand a lack of expression, and on the other hand it is an expression of the fact that resources are not yet mobilized. It is in other words these resources in the individual that should be the focus of treatment.

What is central to and most demanding in this form of treatment is the therapist's hands as well as his/her own respiration and understanding. Psychoanalytical orientation is a part of the treatment.

The therapist's hands in IRT do not treat in a traditional way; they 'listen' and help to create an interaction more than a stimulation.

Johnsen further points out that it may be impossible to train physiotherapists to master this method since Western medicine and Western culture have influenced so much of our education. It has to a certain degree become academic, and by this she means based on theory rather than practical experience. We have also to some extent lost the signals from our inner world; we have become too preoccupied with the outer signals.

Johnsen emphasizes the connection to practice in the following way: 'It has been difficult to describe my work in words, to describe a process that is understood *only* through experience.'

If this can be grasped and acknowledged it will be easier to understand what kind of problems we face when we turn to legitimizing, documenting, and researching in this field. The qualitative aspects, which are at the root of good physiotherapy and good health care, are precisely those aspects we are in danger of losing, or of not finding at all.

CONCLUSION

Colleagues in this book question various aspects of traditional physiotherapy practice. This practice, in general terms, has been largely dualistic, individual and focussed on methods and techniques, usually based on the physiotherapist's own beliefs.

The authors emphasize the importance of acknowledging not

only in theory but also in practice a more holistic approach to patient problems. Such practice must be based on a cooperative dialogue in which the patient's beliefs are acknowledged as legitimate and taken into consideration. The authors further emphasize that a dynamic therapeutic process requires of the physiotherapist, personal self-development, maturity and openness. This represents for many a wider and to some extent new role for the physiotherapist. We hope that the contributions in this book will trigger new discussions about how we should practise physiotherapy, how the field should be developed in the future, and how research and education should be approached in order to ensure the desired development.

REFERENCES

Aalvik J, Willumsen E, Grund J, Vellar O D, Aarø L E 1983 Forebyggende Helsearbeid i 1980-åra, Universitetsforlaget, Oslo
Bunkan B H, Radøy L, Thornquist E 1982 Psykomotorisk behandling Festskrift til Aadel Bülow Hansen. Universitetsforlaget, Oslo
Capra F 1986 Vendepunket. Borgen Forlag, Copenhagen. (1982 The turning point, Simon and Schuster, New York)
Culberg J 1985 Dynamisk psykiatri i teori og praktik. Bokforlaget Natur og Kultur, Sweden
Digregorio V 1984 Rehabilitation of the burn patient. Churchill Livingstone, Edinburgh
Engelsrud G 1985a Kropp og sjel — et dualistisk eller dialektisk forhold? Hovedoppgave, Statens Spesiallærerhøgskole. Bærum, Norway
Engelsrud G 1985b 'Å leve med en livløs kropp — eller å væred en levende kroppen'. Fysioterapeuten 11: 592–600
Helsedirektoratet 1987 Helse for alle i Norge? Kommunalforlaget, Oslo
Hare M 1986 Physiotherapy in psychiatry. William Heinemann Medical Books, London
Hjort P 1982 Norsk Helsepolitikk i 1980 årene. Fysioterapeuten 4: 146–151
Lynch J J 1984 Når hjertet brister, Universitetsforlaget, Oslo (1979 The broken heart, Basic Books Inc, New York)
Mellgren A et al 1983 Psychosomatisk medisin. Bokforlaget Natur og Kultur, Sweden
O'Neill P 1983 Health Crisis 2000. World Health Organization Regional Office for Europe, Copenhagen
Piene R D 1979 Mellom beskjeftigelse og profesion, Hovedfagsoppgave, Institutt for Samfunnsvitenskap, Universitetet i Tromsø, Norway
Risom Petersen J E Løvgren K, Løvgren N-A 1986 Alternativ behandling. Sykepleiersken 21: 26–30

2. Schultz' autogenic training as an individual or group approach in physical therapy: technique or treatment?

K. Denstad

AUTOGENIC TRAINING — RELEVANT IN PHYSICAL THERAPY?

Health services and health professions in the West are faced with complex problems, at the same time as having to cope with an increasing use of the services. Social, economic and psychological problems often lie behind medical diagnoses, and symptoms of emotional disturbance take up an increasing amount of health professionals' time.

This situation brings into focus the question of how physical therapists as a profession are equipped to meet this challenge. Most physical therapists are traditionally trained to treat symptoms rather than seeking the cause of the problems. Even within the limits of their traditional training, physical therapists have choices to make.

First, they may assess and treat symptoms in a local area of the body without regarding the person as a whole; or they may try to understand the symptoms of the individual in a wider context.

Second, they may let the patient remain in a passive role, rather than trying to help him take an active part in improving his own health.

Third, they may choose expensive methods of long duration, or choose methods that do not exclude groups with economic problems from their services.

The use of autogenic training (AT) in physical therapy is closely connected with these professional choices. The main purpose of this chapter is to discuss how the method can be applied and the implications of its use. The term treatment will be used, because AT as a technique is regarded as the essential part of a treatment process. Some theoretical considerations will be presented, but the readers are expected to be familiar with the method. Generally, I have chosen a clinical descriptive approach. Physical therapists who are familiar with the use of AT will agree that the method has several advantages. But for many physical therapists the use of AT raises questions, mostly concerned with its relation to their competence ('Is it legal?') and to its demand for professional expertise ('Is it difficult?'). This chapter also attempts to answer these questions.

But it does not only discuss AT. Views are presented on professional challenges and educational issues concerning the field of psychiatric/psychosomatic physical therapy as a whole. The physiotherapeutic evaluation and the treatment contract (Denstad, 1974) as the basis for therapy planning are regarded as essential in physical therapy in general.

The experience with AT presented in this chapter has been obtained through varied clinical practice in psychiatric and general physiotherapeutic work over a period of 20 years.

Teaching physical therapists AT during their post-graduate education has also provided valuable experience.

THEORETICAL CONSIDERATIONS

The method

Autogenic training was developed in Germany about 1924 by Schultz (1930, 1964) from an interest in studying the effects of autohypnosis. It is interesting to note that the method has only had a limited application in England and USA. One of Schultz' students, however, who moved to Canada, made the literature available in English, and contributed to increased knowledge of the method (Luthe, 1969).

AT has also been called concentrated self-relaxation. It should be noted that the method is regarded as a relaxation technique, and not as hypnosis. According to Norwegian law, hypnosis is reserved for physicians and psychologists. The main difference is that hypnosis is initiated by another person, while AT is completely based on self-instruction. (For general indications for AT see p. 26).

In AT the individual is trained to shift voluntarily from a normal state to a wakeful low-arousal state. The training consists of two series of exercises: standard exercises and meditative exercises.

How meditative exercises may be applied within a special psychotherapeutic context is a task for the psychotherapist, and will not be described in this article. The standard exercises, which include both basic and visceral exercises, are more physiologically oriented, aiming to control muscles, respiration and the circulation system. Only the basic exercises will be included in this presentation. They are the most relevant for physical therapists, and are sufficient to bring a person into an autohypnotic state.

AT, which is a systematically organized method, is based on three main principles:

1. Reduced input of stimuli from outside
2. Mental repetition of psychophysiologically adjusted phrases of selected words (for instance 'right arm is heavy')
3. Passive concentration without strain.

From a comfortable lying or sitting standard position, the individual working on the basic exercises concentrates on calm, then step by step on the feeling of heaviness and warmth in the body. He starts to focus on the feeling of heaviness in the right arm, then proceeds gradually to include both arms, both legs, and finally the body as a whole. Later in the training process when he concentrates on the sensation of warmth in the body, the same procedure is followed. In the course of training, if successful, the sensations will be experienced more rapidly and distinctly. The basic exercises alone usually need 8–12 weeks to work automatically. This indicates that strong motivation is required in AT. The long time needed can be seen as a problem, but in this respect AT — working on concentration and control — follows the same rules as other forms of training. A sportsman starting to train in techniques or build up strength will accept several weeks of intensive work to reach his goal. He will also know that a method not only has to be learnt but also automatized in order to work satisfactorily.

Considerable efforts have been made to investigate the objective effects of relaxation in general, but investigators themselves admit that the results should be taken with a pinch of salt. Benson et al (1974) put forth a hypothesis of the so-called relaxation response as a common denominator for a variety of relaxation methods explaining the altered state of consciousness. 'The relaxation response appears to be an integrated hypothalamic response which results in generalized decreased sympathetic nervous system activity, and perhaps also increased parasympathetic activity. This response, termed the "trophotrop response" ' . . . 'consists of changes opposite to those of the fight or flight response' (the ergotrop response) . . . . 'and are distinctly different from the physiological changes during quiet sitting or sleep'.

From its origin in psychotherapy, AT is today more common in general practice, preventive medicine, odontology and physical therapy (Alnaes & Johnsen, 1968). What is more, practitioners are no longer limited to professionals. Variations of AT have also been introduced on the open market by, for instance, school teachers and sport instructors.

Some aspects connected with the application of AT

Ideomotoric training

The so-called ideomotoric training (Uneståhl, 1982) is aimed at improving the influence of the mind on the body through visualization, in order to enhance the learning of — in this case — AT. It includes practical exercises, such as the pendulum exercise: the person is standing up, eyes closed, holding a pendulum in his hand. He is told to visualize how the pendulum starts to swing, without actually moving it, to paint a mental picture of the movements. This leads to a real movement of the pendulum, gradually more distinct, if the person allows to happen what he wants to happen.

This simple exercise will always bring forth important material in therapy, especially on resistance. If, for instance, the pendulum does not move, and the patient is asked what he was thinking, the answer will give information on his attitude towards the exercise: 'I wondered whether it moved or not', 'I thought that it should move', etc.

In ideomotoric training, concentration on certain images leads to muscular activity. This is both experienced and observed very clearly. The person's attitude towards the task may thus be detected by the therapist, discussed and adjusted. By this procedure he may see the point of passive concentration, which in turn is likely to ensure smooth progress in AT.

The pendulum exercise was also recommended by Schultz and others (Langen & Alnæs, 1964). While some therapists apply such training if the need arises during AT, others work with it as a preparation procedure.

Uneståhl puts considerable weight on ideomotoric training. He sees it as essential to change the situation from one which is experienced as controlled by some 'power' outside the person, to a situation where he himself is in charge.

Physical therapy and psychological mechanisms

Many forms of physical therapy include a high degree of physical contact and often an 'attack' on symptoms: no wonder that resistance and transference phenomena play a great role (Jørstad, 1969) and that dependence between physical therapist and patient can become a problem.

The central issue of psychological mechanisms as influencing powers in physical therapy will only be briefly mentioned. Of importance in this connection is that the intensity of this power will be considerably reduced in AT compared to traditional physical therapy. This is mainly due to the fact that the patient himself takes responsibility for his treatment, and carries it through with the necessary support.

It is interesting to observe, however, that variations in professional leadership in AT influence psychological reactions. The active physical therapist who instructs the patient verbally during the AT exercises, may create a dependence in the patient, a need for instruction from another person in order to succeed; or, on the contrary, a protest at what may be experienced as an intervention in a personal sphere.

Unestähl states that a person during autohypnosis consists of an experiencing and an observing me, and in addition an instructing me. This means that AT involves self-instruction on the part of the patient. This self-instruction complicates the process, because instruction has to do with planning and logic. To facilitate training, the patient is therefore recommended to make the instruction part as automatic as possible. This may be attained by a well-prepared procedure, where the intention of every exercise is made clear, and its content and the awakening well planned. A therapist who is active in the preparing part, and then leaves the patient to self-instruction during the AT exercise, will utterly reduce resistance and transference reactions in the treatment process.

Group treatment

Arranging AT groups has obvious advantages. Although individual goals vary, group members meet for the purpose of learning AT. They will discover that there are others who need help with tension problems and who use the method. They will experience a community where there is 'give and take' between group members. It is also an added advantage that more people can be helped. And a group approach represents a more economic use of time and resources.

The ideal number of members in an AT group depends upon the leader and the way the group is led. 6–10 people may be a suitable number in a therapeutic group based on interaction and individual follow-up.

The group develops its own dynamics. Since a positive group stimulates learning, the significance of clarifying the genuine motivation of the members should be emphasized. One dominating complainer may inhibit the rest of the group with his scepticism.

It is the task of the group leader to stimulate learning and to create an atmosphere of tolerance, where members feel free to share thoughts and feelings. Two quite different elements should preferably be included in the task of the AT group leader:

1. Active instruction, information and advice
2. Attitudes like empathy and attention to the individual as well as to the process in the group as a whole. The leader should know the right time for support, for intervention when the patient's attitude towards AT does not work, or for keeping silent.

The challenge for the leader is to find a balance between these two elements in a therapeutic attitude. I will return to the role of the physical therapist, but further discussion on group dynamics is beyond the scope of this chapter.

Adjusting the relaxation dosage

Helping the patient to adjust the relaxation dosage according to his capabilities is an important task for the therapist. The question of determining the appropriate dosage of relaxation is actualized throughout the whole treatment, but is particularly important in the mid-phase when the warmth exercise is introduced and the effect of relaxation increases.

Some of the reactions during the initial phase of the treatment may be due to new and anxiety-provoking sensations in the body. These reactions will naturally fade with the patient's increased sense of security about what is going on, and about his own ability to control the process. Other unpleasant reactions may be due to overdose as a result of the prolonged duration of each training session, or to the kind of associations the patient may have with calm, heaviness and warmth.

By listening to the patient's reports, the experienced therapist will know when the patient feels uncomfortable with the training. Some further questions generally reveal the reason for the unpleasant experience.

Adjustment of the relaxation dosage is normally a question of instructing the patient to keep to the recommended time of 2−3 minutes, and on occasion even to reduce it. Sometimes a more definite ending to each training session has to be emphasized.

People who object to the short duration of AT usually want more time because of poor concentration. This may be helped by better preparation for the exercises. The patient who feels the need for prolonging his AT session is recommended to separate the actual AT from a rest before and/or after it.

Professional cooperation

Because the causes of psychiatric and somatoform* disturbances are complex in nature, teamwork between professionals is extremely valuable. For the physical therapist it is necessary to know that the patient who is referred for physical therapy has been evaluated as to psychopathology and personal resources as well as somatic conditions.

An optimal cooperation, where physical therapy proceeds in parallel, for instance, with psychotherapy, works as a coordinated treatment where the two processes support each other.

Because of the psychological and physiological changes that occur during AT, the method is regarded as a form of both psychological and medical treatment, regardless of its sometimes rather casual use by non-professionals. The physician is the patient's primary contact: he is often the one who selects and motivates the patient in the first place, and who follows the patient up after the AT is finished. A close cooperation is therefore seen as beneficial to the patient.

---

*According to the DSM-III diagnostic system the term somatoform disorders has replaced psychosomatic disorders. The category includes somatization, conversion, psychogenic pain, hypochondriasis and atypical somatoform disorders.

SELECTION OF PATIENTS

General indications for AT

The indications for using AT are not absolute but vary according to the experience and clinical judgement of the therapist. For the physical therapist the indications for AT will be more limited if she is working alone than if she is part of a team.

Generally, most people will profit from learning relaxation: not only to prevent the development of tension symptoms in their daily lives, but also to improve their ability to obtain complete recreation through relaxation, and to cope with situations where physical or mental control is required.

From our own experience and knowledge from literature, AT is more frequently indicated when the muscular tension state is psychologically based, while it is rarely used in neurological and orthopaedic diseases.

General practitioners spend much time on patients with psychological problems: nervous disturbances are reported to represent 20–30% of the consultations in general practice (Øgar, 1977). A majority of these patients present moderate stress and anxiety symptoms, somatoform or sleeping disturbances. They often get tranquillizers, analgesics and/or physical therapy for their local symptoms. AT may serve as an alternative to tranquillizers and sleeping pills for people who want to work actively to change their habitual reactions, physically as well as emotionally.

It is an advantage if the physician and the physical therapist know each other and have agreed on certain routines for cooperation (Denstad & Guldberg, 1978). Examples of disturbances where cooperation is important are somatoform disorders like migraine headache, or organic diseases like hypertonia. Because of the psychophysiological changes during AT, careful medical control is required for these cases. Patients with sleeping disturbances or symptoms of anxiety and tension as part of a neurotic state may profit from a combination of AT and psychotherapy. The indications for using AT in such cases is rather a question of the patient's willingness and ability to work actively in therapy than the diagnostic label he may have put on him.

There is general agreement in the literature that AT is not advisable for:

— psychotic and borderline patients

— people in acute crises, or on the edge of a nervous
   breakdown
— severe and manifest neurotic states (i.e. anxiety neurosis,
   depressive neurosis, compulsive neurosis).

Equally, AT is of no use for those who get a great deal of
secondary gain from their symptoms, like avoidance of
responsibility, or receiving much attention from others. These
people may express a strong wish to get rid of their symptoms, but
do not really want to change.

To sum up, AT is for relatively healthy people. Nevertheless,
they seek therapy, and have often a history behind them of
symptomatic treatment without any effect.

Selection based on physiotherapeutic evaluation

In order to plan therapy a systematic examination is required.
An examination should fulfil certain requirements. It is
important to get information about the whole body, which
should preferably be examined from different angles (e.g. body
posture, movements, respiration, palpation). The conclusions
drawn from the examination should give the physical therapist
information about the patient's muscular resources and
suitability for treatment. Last but not least, the examination
should be reliable.

Several examination methods have been developed. One
valuable method for use in daily clinical work is the Global
Physiotherapeutic Muscle Examination (GPM) (Sundsvold et al,
1982). This method has been scientifically proved to have a
satisfactory level of reliability. Sundsvold presents GPM in an
article in this series (Sundsvold & Vaglum, 1984) and describes the
method as follows: 'The GPM is a somatic examination which
gives information about muscular status throughout the entire
body, and some aspects of the mental health of the patient: the
possible degree of psychopathology'. The article also describes
'the method of integrating the GPM results with the patient's
somatic and psychological symptoms, social functioning and life
situation in treatment planning'.

Sundsvold points out the significance of evaluating the patient's
need for his tight, painful muscles as part of his defence mechanism
before the therapeutic approach is selected.

Usually, patients are referred to physical therapy for evaluation, with the question of therapy left open. Even if AT is suggested specifically by the physician/psychologist, an independent physiotherapeutic evaluation is recommended. This may lead to other conclusions than AT.

TREATMENT CONTRACT IN PHYSICAL THERAPY

Just as important as choosing a relevant technique in physical therapy is how it is applied, and the way the physical therapist meets the patient. Physical therapy has this in common with psychotherapy. It is essential to come to an agreement with the patient concerning his treatment in the very first encounter between physical therapist and patient. For this purpose the use of a treatment contract is highly recommended. This is mainly because a patient is often referred for physical therapy with no knowledge of its purpose and with no opportunity to decide whether he wishes to undergo such a form of treatment or not. Besides, the patient and the physical therapist often meet each other with different expectations on various levels, primarily concerning the goal of therapy and the way of working together.

After the physical therapy evaluation, a discussion will naturally take place about its results, and whether physical therapy treatment is indicated. First of all, if the patient feels the need for help, it is important to find out what he wants for himself, and to what degree he is willing to invest time, energy and money in order to change. The physical therapist on her part, having gained considerable information about the patient through the evaluation, should give her opinion on the need for treatment and the existing therapeutic alternatives. Together they may discuss a realistic goal for the treatment, as well as the approach to use.

The elements

An ordinary contract includes the following elements:

— the patient's own decision concerning the need or wish for therapy
— agreement on a goal
— content of the treatment, and the sharing of responsibility
— agreement on practical arrangements like frequency and duration of sessions, proposed duration of therapy as a whole, and the fee, if any, to be paid.

Within psychiatric/psychosomatic physical therapy, there are a variety of methods. In those cases where AT is selected as a result of a total evaluation, the training programme and what it includes should be discussed as part of the patient's decision about therapy.

Group therapy is suggested to the patient as the best and most common way of learning the method. But his objections, if any, against joining a group, should of course be respected, and individual treatment be offered as an alternative.

In a group it is important that confidentiality outside the group about other members is agreed on, and also that the patient leaves a message for the group in case of absence, thus contributing to the feeling of security and responsibility.

Sometimes the physical therapy evaluation indicates a need for individual physical therapy of some other kind. This part of the treatment usually precedes AT instead of the two different treatments occurring at the same time. By separating AT from other types of treatment in which the physical therapist may play an active role, the patient is given an opportunity to experience more clearly the effects of his own work.

Defining a goal

Choosing a goal in physical therapy is very important. I will therefore discuss this element of the contract separately. According to Unestähl, there is a circular connection between goal, expectations, achievement and self-image. The point is to define a goal which the patient can achieve, and for which he may mentally prepare himself. If the goal is too easy or too hard to obtain, the achievement will be reduced. Of course, the patient will feel proud and encouraged when one goal is reached. This will in turn lead to more positive expectations concerning his further work towards new goals in AT.

Generally, the defining of goals together with the patient gives the physical therapist an opportunity to relate to the patient as a whole person, and not just focus on the symptoms. It is important that the message of the pain is heard, but the symptom should not have the physical therapist's whole attention. A goal aimed towards an improved achievement ability or a change in habits according to the patient's wish, is preferable to a goal aimed only at getting rid of a symptom. This is especially so when the symptom is well established as part of a neurotic conflict.

An evident and general goal for AT defined by most patients is to learn how to increase their body awareness and practise relaxation in their daily lives. Perhaps they want to use relaxation more specifically in order to:

— be able to take adequate rest periods during their work to prevent the development of tension and pain
— improve their concentration ability in connection with working tasks
— improve the effect of rest and sleep
— reduce anxiety
— discontinue medication like tranquillizers or analgesics.

While such concrete goals may have been set from the beginning, several patients later on report more comprehensive effects from their training, in terms of behavioural changes and an improved relationship with other people.

Through a treatment contract, a more secure and comfortable situation is created both for the patient and for the physical therapist. When the treatment starts, unrealistic expectations are reduced, and the situation is no longer structured by the physical therapist as the only authority, but becomes one of cooperation.

THE TREATMENT PROCESS: CLINICAL EXAMPLES

In the following I want to give a brief survey of the AT process, illustrated by clinical examples. For this purpose the treatment process is divided into four phases, with some of the usual clinical issues covered in each of them:

1. Evaluation phase (which has already been discussed)
2. Initial phase
3. Mid phase
4. Final phase.

For the clinical examples, four categories of patients are described:

1. Patients with stress symptoms (later referred to as stress patient)
2. Patients with psychological problems, able to work actively in psychotherapy (neurotic patient)
3. Patients with moderate tension symptoms, and no evident need for treatment (moderate tension patient)
4. Patients with somatoform disorders and muscular pains (somatoform patient).

The description of each treatment phase will be followed by a clinical example. For practical purposes, the example is connected to the treatment phase which seemed the most significant in that case. Focus will be on an individual development, although the group is referred to.

1. Evaluation phase

Example: stress patient

A 30-year-old man was referred from a general practitioner as a possible candidate for AT. He felt constantly tense, his hands trembling. When he tried to control the trembling, it became even worse. He had also recently suffered from sleep disturbances. He wanted tranquillizers, and was definitely not interested in seeing a psychiatrist. However, when the physician suggested relaxation training as an alternative to medication he was interested.

When I first saw him he was restless and tense. He told me that he lived an extremely busy life both professionally, as a lawyer, and socially. He saw the speed and hyperactivity in his daily life as the root of the problem, giving the following picture of himself: 'My head rushes first, my body comes trailing after'.

He seemed eager to work on his tension problem. A new AT group was just about to start. This left no time for further evaluation such as the GPM. We agreed that he should try to slow down and structure his life while working with AT.

In the group the patient soon presented himself as a rather interested spectator, but was not willing to make a self-commitment. There were always excuses for not following up the training programme at home. However, he found relaxation in the group to be a positive experience, and listened to the reported progress of the others. Towards the end of the treatment sessions, he admitted to the group that he did not really want to work on his problems. Treatment ended after seven group sessions over the course of 8 weeks.

Example illustrates:

— a treatment where the goal was not achieved. The patient was looking for a quick and easy solution to his problems without having to commit himself.
— the result of inadequate preparatory work. If more time and attention had been given to the contract, the lack of

motivation would have been discovered and AT would not
have been started.
— the advantage of a group situation where the relationship
between one's own involvement and the results achieved is
easier to see. It also became clearer to the patient that he
had the opportunity to choose whether he wanted to work
on his problems or not.

2. Initial phase

This phase includes the first and the second AT session. The
treatment contract is worked out individually in advance.

The first session requires a lot of activity on the part of the leader,
and will usually include the following:

— The group members introduce themselves, and state their
goals and expectations.
— The practical arrangement is agreed on. The group
usually meets once a week, seven times, each session
lasting 50–60 minutes.
— A discussion takes place on what AT is, what is going on
mentally and physically during relaxation, why such a
systematic training is required. This discussion is aimed
at creating optimum expectations of the training. At this
stage, the leader's instructions should be short and to the
point, not dwelling on details.
— The nature of passive concentration is explained. Passive
concentration is characterized by an absence of strain. One
neither helps nor prevents things from happening.
— The group is carefully prepared for the training procedure
of the first AT exercise. It is made clear from the first
moment that AT is a silent concentration of the individual
without the verbal instruction of a leader.
— The sitting and lying standard positions are demonstrated,
making sure that the patient is comfortable.
— The first AT exercise is then performed in silence.
— The reactions to the exercise are met and dealt with. It is
essential that each group member is heard and encouraged
in his training at home for the coming week. This will also
help to create a positive atmosphere in the group.
— The group is reminded of the homework assignment: two
minutes of training three times daily in quiet surroundings,

becoming familiar both with the sitting and the lying positions. The same procedure used in the first group exercise is followed.

Second session. This session and all future sessions will be concerned with work on the content of the patients' reports, training, discussion and instructions for further steps in the exercises. The content of the session depends on the material produced by the group.

Repetition of some of the new information given the week before is often asked for, but the main part of the session will naturally be spent on sharing new experiences gained from the home training. The following issues usually require discussion when the leader deals with reactions reported by the patients:

— Emphasis on the patient's own ability to control the process, and his opportunity to choose (I am the one who starts the relaxation, I can choose to stop whenever I wish).
— Standardization of the training procedure. If the individual exercise is well prepared, the training will be simplified and automatization more easily obtained.
— Ideomotoric training. People who 'didn't feel anything' during the exercise are invited to do the pendulum exercise. Attitudes which prevent relaxation such as anxiety, doubt or strain, will then easily be uncovered and can be discussed.
— Adjustment of the relaxation dosage.
— Introduction of simple active relaxation exercises, e.g. stretching or using progressive relaxation principles. Some people prefer to approach AT through active relaxing movements.
— Further individual instruction to find the right balance in the sitting is important, because problems often develop during the day when no bed is at hand.
— As in the first session, the next exercise is planned, then performed in silence. Instructions are given for further training at home.

Example: neurotic patient

A 28-year-old student was referred from a psychologist, with the question of suitability for AT. The patient often felt tense and short of breath, but also felt weak occasionally. As a teenager, she had had anorexia nervosa, which later came under control. She was now undergoing an identity crisis after breaking off her relationship with her boyfriend. GPM showed a quite good muscular status, but indicated quick vacillation and vulnerability. This required a carefully adjusted dosage of relaxation during treatment. The patient wished to learn relaxation, preferably in a group. Her goal was to obtain better control over her breathing, and to allow herself adequate rest periods. There was an agreement with the psychologist that AT was to be combined with psychotherapy.

The patient suddenly became nauseous with the very first instructions in the standard sitting position. The relaxed position of the neck and stomach regions was uncomfortable, and it was threatening for her to release her breath. The meaning of self-control was emphasized; she was to decide when and how much relaxation. Short exercises with definite endings were recommended to her.

She needed close follow-up for a short period of time because of insecurity with regard to her new body sensations. After that, she began to proudly report on her increasing feelings of security and well-being with relaxation. After 4 weeks, she reported a qualitative change in her respiration during AT, 'So deep and quiet without my doing anything special'.

In general she experienced a greater peacefulness and an improved ability to concentrate.

Treatment ended after seven group sessions over the course of 12 weeks.

Example illustrates:

— that it is possible to benefit from AT, despite a difficult life situation, when the environment is secure and treatment occurs in combination with psychotherapy.
— that the initial phase can be decisive. Treatment could have failed if resistive elements had not been handled early. From the very beginning emphasis was placed on creating a safe atmosphere for relaxation. The patient needed information. However, most important was her understanding of her ability to control the process, and the security of determining the appropriate dosage of relaxation.
— that some individuals quickly obtain extensive psychophysiological changes with only the use of basic exercises and a shortened period of AT.
— that psychotherapy and the development of body awareness

can have a mutually stimulating effect. The patient also showed marked progress in psychotherapy during this time.

3. Mid-phase

This phase is characterized by:

— Increased understanding of how to work with AT, and an increased security surrounding the psychophysiological changes which occur during relaxation.
— Realization of a general spreading of calm and heaviness in the body. Warmth exercise is trained. The group members advance at their own pace.
— Increased contact with the body as a whole.
— Growing independence. Individual patterns of AT develop from the standard exercises.
— Achievements. Some goals are reached. Goals are discussed.
— Increased contact with and control of individual problems in AT, such as achievement tension, anxiety, impatience, poor structuring, failing motivation.
— Discussion of one's feelings about having come half-way through the treatment.
— More responsibility taken over by the group members, for each other and for what is going on in the group. Less intervention is required from the leader.

Example: moderate tension patient

A 25-year-old student was referred from a general practitioner, complaining of pain and stiffness in his shoulders and neck. This together with some sleep disturbances had begun some months earlier when he had passed an exam under considerable strain. However, he had not felt the expected relief when the exam was over.

When we met, the patient was interested in a muscle examination, but showed mixed feelings about adopting the role of patient. As the GPM showed a rather good muscular status, I could confirm his feelings on this point: the need for treatment was not evident. But what about learning relaxation in a group? The patient showed an immediate interest in this suggestion, as the examination had revealed to him his reduced body awareness. The main goal for him was to train his ability to relax.

The patient followed the training, and actively participated in the group. However, progress was slow. He made no attempt to hide his disappointment over his lack of progress.

Half-way through the treatment he indicated that the more he needed relaxation the worse it went with AT. He tried the pendulum exercise in the group. This clearly showed that the patient anxiously awaited the results of each exercise. He was helped to understand the meaning of passive concentration. This understanding was the turning point in the treatment. He later proudly told of his rapid progress and how his increased relaxation had had a significant effect on his muscular problems.

At the time treatment ended, he was satisfied with his greater ability to relax when the need arose and with his increased body awareness.

Treatment ended after eight group sessions over the course of 3 months.

The example illustrates:

— that patients who could have managed without treatment and who are sceptical about the traditional patient role can benefit considerably from AT.
— a treatment where the turning point came half-way through the process. In the beginning, progress was hindered by anxious expectations of good results. Treatment could easily have failed at this point. It was decisive that the patient received help in overcoming this resistance and in understanding the nature of passive concentration.
— that use of relatively small therapeutic resources can provide adequate help to the patient in the prevention of future problems and in an increased feeling of well-being.

4. Final phase

Completion of treatment should always be well prepared. When there is a treatment contract, the completion of treatment is prepared from the very beginning.

It may help to sharpen the patient's own activity by reminding him of how much time is left. One could, for instance, ask how he feels about being half-way through the treatment. The issue of ending the therapy will also occur during the treatment when physical therapist and patient discuss progress and problems in connection with the patient's goal.

In the final phase the results of treatment are evaluated. However, one last therapeutic procedure may be recommended at this point: reinforcement of the therapeutic value of the basic exercises by concentrating on a specially chosen phrase. This phrase, which is given a short, precise and positive form, is added to the standard formula. It is chosen according to the patient's wishes for change. He may wish to carry through a diet, to control his anxiety, or to work on inhibiting characterological traits within a psychotherapeutic frame of reference. It can be formed by the patient alone, by the help of the group, or with his psychotherapist if psychotherapy occurs simultaneously.

At the end of treatment, it is natural for the group members to discuss how they feel about going on by themselves. If the group wishes to maintain contact over a longer period of time, the last sessions can be held at longer intervals.

Example: somatoform patient

A 45-year-old office worker was referred from a general practitioner because of restless sleep and occasional hyperventilation. The physician sent information concerning a complicated medical history: hypertension, angina pectoris and a cardiac infarct 6 years prior, frequent tension headaches and a previous history of migraine headache. Local physical therapy of the neck had made him worse. He had been an inpatient at a psychiatric clinic 15 years earlier, but did not feel the need for psychiatric treatment at the time. In addition to his antihypertensive medication, the patient was also taking analgesics for headaches, along with tranquillizers.

The physician referred him for evaluation, questioning whether I had anything to offer a patient suffering from anxiety/tension at night and disabling headaches during the day. GPM indicated a moderately good muscular status with little body awareness. The condition seemed firmly established.

AT came into the discussion because the patient felt that he needed help in learning to take better care of his body. He was frightened by the amount of medication he was using for headaches. He set discontinuation of both tranquillizers and analgesics as his primary goal. Medical control was necessary during treatment because of his hypertension and his prior history of migraine headaches.

The patient followed the training conscientiously. He needed considerable time to become comfortable in the standard positions, and was not sure if he was relaxed or not. He felt that he achieved better contact with his body when he began AT with active relaxation exercises which had been introduced to the group. Progress was very slow, and reflected his poor relationship with his body. He just barely felt the effects of AT.

Towards the end of treatment he reported that this concentration and the results he achieved were better in the group situation than at home. We found that the difficulty was in planning an exercise, and he received help with it.

The turning point came at the last treatment session. The patient had attained a noticeably better level of concentration under AT, and told of the 'great tranquillity and restfulness in body and heart' under relaxation. He admitted that he had doubted his ability to manage AT. He didn't feel ready to discontinue treatment, and we agreed on two individual treatments at one month intervals. Considerable changes occurred during this time. His increased contact with his respiration allowed him to break the vicious circle between anxiety and breathing problems at night. Sleep improved and became more peaceful, and his headaches were markedly decreased. Use of analgesics and tranquillizers was reduced to a minimum. The patient began to bicycle. This had a positive effect on his blood pressure.

Treatment ended after nine treatments over a course of 5 months.

Example illustrates:

— that somatoform disorders require medical control under AT.
— that it is possible to define a goal for AT despite a
   complicated medical history — in this case the
   discontinuation of medication.
— that there is a marked individual difference in the amount of
   time required to obtain results. Progress was extremely slow
   for this patient despite his patient efforts. It was only at the
   end of the treatment that he managed to formulate a
   problem with which he could be helped. Concentration
   improved through the use of a more standardized
   procedure. Considerable changes then occurred.
— the importance of a flexible treatment procedure.
   Combined group and individual treatment can be
   advantageous, as well as re-evaluation of a treatment
   contract underway with regard to a continuation.

— that relative to goals set, a minimal use of therapeutic resources can give beneficial results in a situation where symptoms are fairly incapacitating and engrained. This patient was able to eliminate a vicious circle and experience increased well-being and initiative through better body awareness and control.

CHALLENGES TO THE TRADITIONAL ROLE OF THE PHYSICAL THERAPIST

Working with AT represents challenges to physical therapists in several ways, mainly regarding their own professional development. In the post-graduate education courses, where physical therapists are trained to use AT in physical therapy, these challenges are often discussed.

In the following, some of these issues will be presented. Some of them will probably be recognized by physical therapists who have expanded their traditional role in psychiatric/psychosomatic physical therapy.

The main challenge reported by physical therapists seems to be that the AT process is based on a verbal communication between physical therapist and patient, where psychological mechanisms in the interpersonal relationship become more important. The treatment has characteristics in common with psychotherapy, which has made many physical therapists ask whether AT is within their field of competence.

This dialogue covers the interview in the evaluation phase, the forming of a treatment contract, and the AT process itself.

Physical therapists seem to be familiar with their role as interviewer, but express a lack of knowledge about how to communicate with the patient about the content of the contract, and about the treatment process. They often feel insecure when they are not using their hands, applying familiar methods or using the usual physiotherapeutic equipment. The important question is how to make the dialogue function as a therapeutic process.

A therapeutic dialogue implies that the physical therapist — without losing therapeutic control of the situation — accepts and actively uses the patient's capability and motivation to take responsibility for his own situation. How to balance this is often considered a problem.

One of the tasks of the AT therapist is to balance on the one hand the active instruction required in the treatment, and on the other hand the ability to listen to and wait for the patient, giving him the chance to find his own solutions. Physical therapists are trained to conduct, give the answers, maintain authority. It is not surprising that a feeling of insufficiency is often reported when they have to practise a listening, empathic attitude.

Other aspects of the therapeutic attitude may also be seen as a challenge. It is, for instance, important to support and encourage what the patient has already experienced as positive in AT. But the physical therapist should at the same time be able to identify and work on the resistance phenomena, which can prevent the patient's further progress if they are not dealt with.

The use of AT may imply a new way of evaluating changes in the course of the treatment. While physical therapy is traditionally aimed at reducing local symptoms, AT will often aim at behavioural changes, e.g. an improved achievement ability.

It seems to be quite a challenge for physical therapists to practise AT in groups. Most of them lack training in this type of group therapy, and feel insecure about how a group should be composed, and how to organize and lead it.

Finally, a more practical problem should be mentioned. The physical therapist who works with AT will find that she needs to organize her work environment differently. A quiet, separate room is required, undisturbed by telephone calls, etc. The physical therapist has to be physically present and mentally with the patient.

This list of challenges indicates that physical therapists may find working with AT an unsettling and unusual experience. Therefore, I want to emphasize the simplicity of the method. Because the use of AT is essentially different from traditional physical therapy, it is necessary that physical therapists train themselves, and expand their field of competence. However, the special training required does not have to be extensive.

QUALIFYING PHYSICAL THERAPISTS FOR AT

It is the task of post-graduate education to enable physical therapists to expand their field of competence. In the following I first describe an educational model for physical therapists who want to work with AT in physical therapy, a course which is available for physical therapists in any kind of physiotherapeutic practice. I then present some ideas on education concerning the whole field of psychiatric/psychosomatic physical therapy.

The recommended extra professional training may take

different forms. I have personal experience of an educational model of short duration — six sessions in a course of 3 months — which appears to have worked. In addition to conveying knowledge in a traditional way, this course emphasizes the physical therapists' personal experiences through learning and practising AT themselves. Gradually they learn how to select patients for AT, how to form a contract including a goal for the treatment, and how to facilitate the AT process. By sharing personal experiences and discussing patient reports, the group of physical therapists will supply each other with clinical material, which will be valuable to them in further treatments. The physical therapists are recommended to limit AT to the basic exercises, at least in the beginning. Therapeutic problems, and the challenges which I just referred to, are discussed in the group. The physical therapists may thus learn to cope with them in a new way. One important aspect is that the course with its 15 physical therapists also forms a therapeutic group situation in itself. The physical therapists are trained in leadership tasks in front of the group. Some of them feel encouraged to start small groups of patients before the course is ended.

It is of great importance that physical therapists who use AT in therapy have personal experience of the method and are able to behave in a relaxed way in front of the patient. Even subtle non-verbal signs of insecurity in front of the patient may be noticed by him, and spoil both his confidence and his relaxation.

Cooperation with a psychotherapist or a general practitioner is an important part of the learning process, as is supervision from a more experienced professional. Supervision is also a valuable support if the physical therapist experiences personal problems during the process. If, for instance, the reactions from a patient or a group make the physical therapist feel insecure, it is reassuring to know there is a place where problems can be discussed and thereby handled in a more constructive way.

Qualifying physical therapists for work within the whole field of psychiatric/psychosomatic physical therapy is an extensive educational task.

The professional qualifications can be developed through both theoretical knowledge and increased self-knowledge and body awareness of the physical therapist.

The professional knowledge which is required is not restricted to physical therapy. There is a need for relevant knowledge in psychiatry and psychology.

Instruction about how to establish a working relationship between physical therapist and patient should also be included in the education.

I also see a need for the physical therapist to improve her skill in verbal communication. Learning how to make the dialogue function as part of a therapeutic process will increase her sense of security in the therapeutic situation.

As part of professional knowledge, an increased body awareness is important. Awareness of the body, i.e. coming into contact with one's own breathing, body feelings and body language, will develop the sensitivity of the physical therapist as a therapeutic tool, and her ability to be present in the relationship with the patient. A higher degree of awareness about her own attitudes and what is going on interpersonally during therapy is most surely attained when the physical therapist herself has gone through psychotherapy.

CONCLUSION

This paper presents one view on the application of AT in physical therapy.

The importance of spending time on the selection and evaluation of patients prior to the actual start of AT is emphasized. Some readers may consider this part of the treatment less significant. My experience is that the small investment of time spent by physical therapist and patient at this stage of therapy gives considerable gains.

While several reports show that only about 50% of those who start AT complete the treatment, it is my experience that only a very small number drop out. I feel convinced that these different experiences reflect different approaches to AT, i.e. whether it is considered a technique, or seen as an essential part of a treatment process based on adequate preparatory work.

One important aspect of this method is that it gives the patient responsibility for his own treatment. It may also give the patient encouraging results after a short period of time, in terms of achievement ability, self-confidence and increased awareness of the body as a whole.

What makes AT such an interesting method is that a brief standard instruction opens up a variety of individual responses. It is of critical importance, however, that the physical therapist has developed the ability to be in a therapeutic dialogue with the patient, and knows how to help him to overcome the resistance phenomena which may occur during treatment. This seems a major task in the education of physical therapists for applying AT in their work.

In AT the amount of therapeutic input is small compared to the time spent. The treatment therefore — especially when practised in groups — represents a small expense both for the patient and for health insurance.

Physical therapists are increasingly confronted with psychosocial problems in their work. A method such as AT should become one of the standard treatments which physical therapists are trained to use.

REFERENCES

Alnæs R, Johnsen G 1968 Psykoterapi II Metoder. Fabritius, Oslo
Benson H, Beary J F, Carol M P 1974 The relaxation response. Psychiatry 37: 37–46
Denstad K 1974 Contract in physiotherapy. Proceedings of the World Confederation for Physical Therapy, Montreal
Denstad K, Guldberg A 1978 Autogen trening i almenpraksis. Journal of the Norwegian Medical Association 27: 1327–1328
Jørstad J 1969 Overføring og motoverføring i psykoterapi og fysioterapi. Mensendieckbladet 4: 3–15
Langen D, Alnæs R 1964 Avspenning ved konsentrasjon. Fabritius, Oslo
Luthe W 1969 Autogenic therapy. Grune & Stratton, New York
Øgar B 1977 Pasienter i norsk almenpraksis. Universitetsforlaget, Oslo
Schultz J H 1930 Uber das autogene Training. In: Würzburger Abhandlungen aus d. Gesamtgebiet d. Medizin. Neue Folge. Kabitzsch, Leipzig
Schultz J H 1964 Das autogene Training. (Mainwork, 11 edition.) Thieme, Stuttgart, pp 431
Sundsvold M Ø, Vaglum P 1984 Muscular pains and psychopathology. In: Hoskins Michel T (ed) International perspectives in physical therapy: volume on pain. Churchill Livingstone, London
Sundsvold M Ø, Vaglum P, Denstad K 1982 Global fysioterapeutisk muskelundersøkelse. Til bruk i Klinisk arbeid og forskning. Eget forlag, Oslo, pp 211
Uneståhl L E 1982 Hypnos i teori och praktik. Veje, Ørebro

3. Psychomotor therapy: an approach to the evaluation and treatment of psychosomatic disorders

B. H. Bunkan & E. Thornquist

HISTORY

Psychomotor therapy *ad modum* Braatøy and Bülow-Hansen is a branch of physiotherapy that has developed in Norway. It is the result of cooperation between two people with different professional backgrounds: Braatøy was a psychiatrist and Bülow-Hansen was, and still is, a physiotherapist.

In the course of her clinical work, Bülow-Hansen treated tense patients suffering from unspecific dorsalgias, tension headaches, arm pain caused by writing etc. She noticed that none of the forms of treatment of muscular tension she applied had any effect unless they involved breathing. She also noticed that while local, symptom-oriented treatment was of great help to some patients, it was none at all to others. Some even grew worse. She began to question these results and became convinced that the differences were linked with differences in respiration. People with relatively free and versatile breathing responded well to local treatment, while most of those with neck and shoulder stiffness, general tension problems, and problems of dysfunction obtained no relief if their breathing was restricted and controlled. She tried out various methods and discovered how to influence and use respiration to regulate the degree of relaxation. She was also aware that the whole body had to be treated if the effects of the treatment were to be lasting, because changes in one place always have widespread effects in the rest of the body. Trygve Braatøy became interested in her experiences. He had never come across this way of thinking in a physiotherapist before. Braatøy himself was interested in all aspects of psychiatry and among Norwegian doctors was the one with the clearest understanding of the body's significance for psycho-emotional change and personal growth. Braatøy (1947, 1954) describes body-oriented psychotherapy in his own patients.

These books deal with central themes in psychotherapy, and several cases are described in the light of body-oriented therapy. Braatøy was well-informed and widely read, and his description of this form of treatment in '*De Nervøse* Sinn' (1947) includes references to theories and techniques from the work of Jacobson, Schultz, Reich, Pavlov, Kempf, Ferenszi, Roemheld and many others.

New ideas in physiotherapy

Psychomotor therapy differed considerably from traditional physiotherapy and there was a great deal of resistance to it during the 40s and 50s.

What distinguished psychomotor therapy was its emphasis on the whole person, and especially its treatment of the body as an integrated whole (Thornquist & Bunkan, 1986; Øvreberg & Andersen, 1986). Symptoms were regarded as a sign that something was wrong with the whole body, so they were not specially treated at all. When the entire body had been thoroughly worked over the painful symptoms were relieved.

A second distinguishing factor was the idea of the close relation between the body and emotions and feelings. Our feelings are transmitted through and reflected in our bodies. In psychomotor therapy breathing and feelings are regarded as being interdependent, and treatment of breathing became one of the central aspects. When the breathing patterns altered, the patients began to react emotionally, and conflicts and forgotten feelings rose to the surface. Many patients also found that their senses became sharper: smell, sight and hearing improved and sense perceptions became clearer.

During the treatment process changes in posture and movement pattern usually occurred spontaneously, without any direct, specific corrections having to be made. Autonomic and hormonal functions also tended to normalize: digestion improved, menstruation became regular, and so on. These physical changes were accompanied by and inseparable from psychological changes. Thus psychomotor therapy gradually became an extension of psychotherapy.

The ideology and the approach on which psychomotor therapy

was based were outside the experience of and incomprehensible to most doctors and physiotherapists. Psychomotor therapy today attracts a great deal of interest in Norway and Scandinavia generally.

FRAMEWORK OF UNDERSTANDING

Attitude towards the body

Psychomotor therapy is based on the well-known theory that the organism functions as a whole. The method recognizes that:

— the body is a functional and interacting entity
— psyche and soma are indivisible.

No sharp lines are drawn between emotional/psychological and physical reactions. A person's reaction involves the whole of him, and cannot be subdivided in any way. There is no real division between mind and body; a person is always both at the same time.

Artificial barriers have been erected between the body's various organs and functions. Motor, autonomic, respiratory and hormonal reactions are usually thought of and treated separately and independently. In psychomotor therapy, however, these barriers are broken down and emphasis is laid on the fact that the body's various functions influence one another, and that disturbances in one place affect the equilibrium of the entire body.

All bodily functions interact in a reciprocal way. The body does not consist of a series of states, but of interdependent processes. It is dynamic, not static.

The therapeutic consequences of this way of thinking are that the physiotherapist continually registers all bodily reactions and relates individual reactions and findings to the person's whole life situation.

These two fundamentally different approaches can be briefly characterized as follows:

'Separatist' approach	*Psychomotor therapy*
Body as machine	Combination of interacting organs and functions
Separate parts/fragments	Reciprocity/interaction
Static condition	Dynamic processes
Simple cause and effect	Complex causal relations/complex reactions

| Repair the fault/local treatment | Treat the whole body/whole person |
| Mind and body two separate entities | Mind and body inseparable. |

The psychomotor therapy approach breaks with the traditional medical view of the body. It is not a question of *adding on* a psychosocial dimension to the biologically oriented, mechanical concept of the body. It is a question of a qualitatively different way of thinking.

Emphasis on breathing

Any observant clinician will have experienced to what extent breathing indicates and regulates the emotions.

To a great extent our breathing affects and is affected by our feelings. The fact that respiration is the barometer of a person's emotional state means that practitioners of psychomotor therapy regard it as:

— the best of all diagnostic aids
— the best guide as to how to proceed during a treatment session.

When physiotherapists talk of respiration, they are usually referring to a pathological condition in the medical sense: bronchitis, emphysema, atelectasis, lung fibrosis, etc. In psychomotor therapy, however, the importance attached to the way the patient breathes is derived from an understanding of the role breathing plays in regulating our feelings, and vice versa.

What does a person do when he does not want or dare to show that he feels rejected, upset, disappointed? He 'holds his breath and clenches his teeth'. This is how feelings are held in check by inhibited breathing and muscular tension. This is how we suppress feelings whose expression we and our surroundings find unacceptable.

Restricted breathing is a significant element in suppression of feelings

In a frightening situation we all hold our breath. Not until we feel secure again do we release it in a sigh of relief.

There is a dynamic interaction between emotions and respiration. Just as we express our feelings via respiration, so we are able to hold threatening feelings and impulses in check via respiration. To breathe freely is to allow feelings full expression; to breathe in a restricted way is to hold them back. Awareness of this *interaction* is essential in psychomotor therapy, which makes use of it therapeutically.

The following examples show how we emphasize the role of respiration in practice.

When we palpate muscles, for example, we are just as interested in the person's breathing responses to our grip as we are in what we feel beneath our fingertips.

— Does the person hold his breath when we press tender
  muscles?
— Or does he spontaneously gasp and say 'Ow!'?

These reactions indicate the person's general reaction pattern: whether he keeps things back or expresses his feelings.

We also note the versatility of the person's breathing in relation to the position and posture of the body:

— Is the breathing more restricted and controlled (in a
  negative sense) when the person is lying on his back than
  when he is standing up?

In the same way, when we carry out functional tests we register respiratory responses to the same extent as, for example, range of movement:

— When the person gapes, does his breath flow freely through
  the thorax, does it stop in the thorax, or does he hold his
  breath?

The versatility and spontaneity of the breathing tells us about the adaptability and spontaneity of the person.

Respiration at a given moment and over time

We take note not only of the patient's respiration at the time, but also its long-term effects on the body. The time aspect of respiration is important and has considerable consequences for therapy.

When feelings are held in check over a long period the breathing will affect the body in various ways. Respiratory inhibition mechanisms can affect the position of the thorax and lead to reduced mobility and stiffness of parts of the thorax.

Active expiration is a characteristic way of breathing when

feelings are being tightly controlled. Given the form and function of the primary respiratory muscles, the abdominal muscles, and the latissimus dorsi, it is obvious that a person's way of breathing will in time affect not only the thorax, but also the weight-bearing and centre of balance of the whole body. Since the respiratory bellow is more or less in the centre of the body, breathing patterns become part of the individual's characteristic posture and movement pattern (Thornquist, 1983; Bunkan, 1985).

Yawning

A complete yawn gives a good idea of the degree of respiratory inhibition. Where there is free respiration the yawn triggers the impulse for inspiration, with movements that run through the whole thorax including the apex. Yawning is a very clear illustration of the connection between the state of muscular tension and the breathing function. *Muscular tension and respiration are mutually restricting and mutually liberating.* This fits in with what we have observed about breathing and emotions. When we hold our breath from fear there is always an increase in muscular tension. The shoulders are raised and the body adopts a flexed attitude. When the danger is over, not only is there a sigh of relief, but the shoulders go down and the muscles relax. The breathing response and the muscular response occur simultaneously. How, then, does yawning affect the relation between breathing and musculature?

A complete yawn opens the face and triggers an impulse of extension and abduction throughout the body. A good yawn requires adequate muscular and respiratory flexibility. The more a person uses his muscles to put brakes on his feelings, the greater the resistance to the liberating stretching and respiratory impulses of the yawn.

In tense people, for example, one may see the yawning movement spread from the jaw to cautious extension movements of the arms, while the fingers remain slightly flexed. The stretching is not allowed to reach the fingertips or toes and there is no stretching of the whole body. Whether and how the stretching and respiratory impulses of the yawn spread through and establish themselves in the body provides important information about a person's general state of tension and thus about his emotional checks and controls.

Because a yawn is so visible and so easy to observe it is a good aid to the assessment of physical and consequently emotional blocks.

Bodily changes and feelings

Bodily changes — the loosening of muscular and respiratory restraints — involve the liberation of feelings.

How much release of muscular tension and respiratory liberation can a person tolerate? How far can we go in stimulating a free stretching of the body? Respiration is always the therapist's signal as to how much change the patient can bear. When the tension in the thorax lessens and the breathing becomes freer, the patient may begin to cry. When stretching impulses spread through the body, suppressed feelings may rise to the surface, like fear or dammed-up anger. If release of muscular tensions is not accompanied by freer breathing, there will be no physical or emotional changes. To obtain a free stretch in the body — an erect, relaxed posture and free, flexible movements — the breathing must be liberated. If a person holds his breath during treatment this tells us that he has reservations. That he wants to retain control. As we mentioned above, respiration is the barometer of our emotional state.

The patient's respiration therefore has to be continually registered as a guide during the treatment. The therapist needs to be constantly attentive and aware in order to regulate the amount of muscular and respiratory treatment she gives. The more the respiration is liberated, the more profound the effect of the treatment. It is therefore very important to allow scope for feelings during the treatment. Emotional reactions can be a sign of health — an expression of contact with and acceptance of one's own feelings. If we as therapists do not allow the patient to express his feelings, we hinder the process of change in the body and thus in the whole person.

Expansion of the 'whole body' view

We are all subject to the law of gravity and to our feelings at the same time. Our emotional state at any moment and over time determines *how* gravity affects our body. When we are sad and resigned the body involuntarily sinks into a flexed position, which is reinforced by the force of gravity. Everything a human being experiences is impressed on the body, including our experiences as social beings, i.e. non-physical events also find physical expression in our bodies.

It is no coincidence that many expressions that describe fundamental personality traits have physical origins. How should we interpret tension in the calves and feet and 'clinging to a support'? 'To cling to' means 'to resist separation from', to be unable to stand alone, on one's own feet — not to trust one's own feet. If one is afraid of losing one's footing, literally and metaphorically, one is not an independent person in the literal meaning of the word, since the Latin *dependere* means 'to hang down from'.

'To stand back' and 'on tiptoe' indicate reserve and distance, and enthusiasm and restlessness, respectively, but isolated observations must be treated with care. The context is essential, and the therapist must find the patterns in the tensions, weight-bearing and balance of the whole body.

What has life taught us about the psychological or emotional meaning of particular patterns of movement and posture? We have all experienced, for example, that flexion and adduction contractions are a defensive measure. Flexion and adduction are the immediate response to fright, together with holding the breath. We breath a sigh of relief and relax the tense flexion–adduction posture when the danger is over.

— Free movement presupposes that we have released our flexion–adduction tensions.
— Free movement presupposes that we dare to surrender control over our breathing.

Free extension — free stretch in the body — should not be confused with *active* extension — the straight back no matter what, used by the person who is 'pulling himself together'. Emotions can be held in check by tense extension as well as tense flexion, even though these appear to be opposite patterns of reaction. They both have the same psychological function, which is to restrain feelings. Releasing the tensions caused by flexion or extension means surrendering control, letting go of and letting out pent-up feelings.

Being in a state of equilibrium

The ideal body is in a state of what we can call mobile *equilibrium*. It is stable and steady and at the same time flexible and elastic. It requires little muscular effort to carry out movements or maintain a position. All the body's various segments are balanced against each other in a way that is both free and stable. For freedom and movability are not opposites of stability and balance; the states are interdependent. Such a body is usually strong and resilient and can bear more strain than a stiffer body. It can call upon reserves of strength, or relax into a resting position according to the situation and requirements. In other words, the ideal body is versatile and adaptable. There are no unreleasable blocks, and movements can spread freely and without obstruction through the body. These two factors are inseparable: a good equilibrium involves physical and psychological balance.

A healthy person also has good contact with the body as a whole and with parts of it, and has an intact body awareness and consciousness.

Consequently this person has good emotional contact and a body that is fully alive and functioning.

All physiotherapists agree that a state in which excessive muscular work is required to maintain the body in any position is undesirable. The same applies to excessive muscular work used to carry out movements, which leads to poor coordination, with negative consequences for body flow and rhythm. Recognition of the interplay between muscles, breathing and feelings implies new ways of evaluating and treating posture, movement and all forms of bodily dysfunction.

When the patient with low back stiffness and inhibited respiration becomes upset and restless during the treatment, what conclusions do we draw? When his back muscles and his respiration begin to loosen up, his defences begin to give way. He loses control over his unresolved feelings, his suppressed memories, his unfulfilled desires. Emotional reactions are part of the physical processes of change, but if the reactions are very strong and appear to inhibit function, the therapist must ask herself whether her treatment has decreased the muscular and respiratory defences too much. Has she been considerate enough, sensitive enough, to the patient's reactions during the treatment and between sessions? She must also consider whether to invite the patient to involve a psychiatrist or psychologist. When the psychiatrist/psychologist has evaluated the situation, she, the therapist and the patient can agree on a programme of treatment.

It is important to remember that physical patterns of defence can remain in the body long after the situation that initiated them is over. Braatøy (1947) called this 'the jamming phenomenon'. Once a person has worked through and resolved his emotional traumas, he no longer needs his physical defence mechanisms. They no longer serve any purpose; on the contrary, they are an impediment, physically speaking, and can lead to secondary dysfunction. If these physical changes are great enough, they may also be emotionally inhibiting. Muscular tension and restricted breathing, for example, not only hold feelings in check, they also effect general receptivity. The body shuts off its own feelings and also the rest of the world. Sense impressions and awareness of surroundings are muffled. When the patient responds to the release of tension and breathing with a subjective feeling of relief and we register no physical resistance, this often indicates that the patient's symptoms are caused by mechanical or 'jamming' phenomena.

It is important to remember, however, that the body is also a biological and physical entity in the sense that muscular tension and patterns of posture and movement can have purely somatic causes. Injuries, mechanical pressure, operations, and illnesses can all give rise to reflex muscle contractions, which in turn may lead to ineffective movements and motor habits.

The physiotherapist's task is to diagnose problems relating to movement and to distinguish the mechanical and psychosocial causes. In order to do this, she must have grasped the essence of psychomotor therapy:

— Clinical findings must not be added together, but seen in relation to each other, compared and evaluated.
— Respiration is the most important indicator on which to base a professional opinion because of its role in the regulation of feelings.
— Clinical findings and clinical evaluations must be seen in relation to the person's whole life situation.

INDICATIONS FOR PSYCHOMOTOR THERAPY

In psychomotor therapy we concentrate on the person's total functioning, flexibility, and adaptability, irrespective of symptoms and diagnosis.

The title of this article raises the question of the nature of psychosomatic disorders.

'Psychosomatic medicine is a paradox invented in an honest attempt to re-establish a total view in medicine', as a Norwegian psychiatrist has so penetratingly said. In classical medicine the term psychosomatic is used for disorders where somatic, structural changes are observable, but where psychological factors are regarded as playing a considerable role. This means that, for example, stomach ulcers are considered to be psychosomatic while general tension is not. This is obviously meaningless. The fact that some diseases are characterized as psychogenic and not others illustrates the extent to which dualism and the fragmented view of the body and the person dominate medicine in our culture.

The indications for psychomotor treatment used to be all types of afflictions caused by strain, but above all muscular afflictions. But during the 30 to 40 years it has been practised, it has been shown to have a beneficial effect on constipation, menstrual pain, problems of sexual function, and so-called psychosomatic disorders like bronchial asthma and essential hypertension, as well as afflictions and dysfunction in the musculoskeletal system (Bunkan et al, 1982).

A prerequisite for psychomotor therapy is a capacity for physical and emotional change. Thus, the treatment is not necessarily suitable for everyone with musculoskeletal disorders caused by strain. The aim of the treatment is to bring about a process of change in the body, starting with posture, muscles and breathing. Since this is accompanied by a process of emotional change, it requires certain psychological resources to cope with it; the patient needs ego-strength.

The therapist has to assess the suitability of the method for each patient, and she does this by giving him a full physical examination. Whatever the diagnosis, we cannot judge whether a person will be able to take full advantage of the process of physical change that psychomotor therapy implies without this. The limiting factors may be physical and/or psychological. Physical factors would be fixation of the lumbar vertebrae, arthrodesis of the hip and other joints, etc. In these cases there are mechanical barriers to changes in posture, muscular tension and breathing.

At the other end of the scale are psychotic patients, whose limits are emotional and psychological. This type of person usually lacks the capacity for emotional change and consequently for the physical changes that psychomotor therapy aims at. A third group that is not considered suitable are those in a difficult social or personal situation who need all their defences in order to continue to function.

Between these extremes it is the therapist's responsibility to find out who is likely to benefit from treatment. When we say that psychomotor therapy is not suitable for psychotic patients, we mean the method in its classical form, since the principles and way of thinking are applicable to most forms of emotional problems. The situation is very different, however, when the psychomotor therapist is working with a psychologist or psychiatrist. The physical and verbal approaches can function extremely well together when the two professionals have the same treatment goals and a similar assessment of the patient. When tensions relax and breathing is liberated, dammed-up feelings and unresolved conflicts often rise to the surface. The treatment of the body provided by the physiotherapist can in this case strengthen and support the active working-through process. During other phases the physiotherapy can be used to develop the person's body awareness and to stabilize the body and thus the person, rather than to bring about change. This helps the patient to function in the particular situation he is in at the time.

COMPLETE PHYSICAL EXAMINATION

Posture

We examine the posture and bearing of the body in several different positions in order to get an idea of the person's habit patterns and ability to change.

— How does the person appear? How does he move, use his body, make use of himself?

In order to answer this question, we have to analyse the posture and bearing in detail, and ask ourselves the following types of questions:

— How does the person stand on his feet?
— Does he use much muscular strength to keep upright?
— Is there agreement between the upper and lower parts of the body? Between the right and left sides?
— Is his characteristic posture more flexed or more extended?
— Is the flexion active or passive— is he hunched together or slack?
— Is the extension pattern active or passive?

We place the person in different positions and compare our findings:

— Does the body show the same characteristics when standing as when lying?
— In a standing position, do the characteristics become more, or less, pronounced?

When lying on the back the posture muscles may become more pliant for mechanical reasons. If the shoulders protract more and the neck lordosis increases, this can have emotional connotations.

Functional tests

The body's flexibility is the central point here. Muscular contraction over time leads to shortening of the muscles and surrounding tissue. Contraction and short muscles prevent free movement and hinder the natural flow of accompanying movements through the body. The ideal body is so flexible that every movement sends a ripple through it. Movement and stretching impulses have full scope. In any examination we are therefore interested in finding out as much as possible about how and why there are blocks and how free movement and free function are held in check.

— What sort of equilibrium is there between the various muscle groups as regards length and tension?
— Is there any pronounced tension and shortening of the flexors, the muscles we associate with primitive defence mechanisms?
or
— Does the person give an impression of control and concealment, i.e. does he make most use of the extensors? People with reduced extensibility or length of the extensors usually also have shortened flexors with reduced extensibility. In other words the person is stiff and on the defensive.
— What sort of capacity for relaxation does the person have? Is he able to, i.e. does he dare, surrender control, or is it a learned and voluntary relaxation?
— Is the person aware of his own muscular tension in an activity? In other words, is he conscious of his body, or has he alienated himself from it?

All forms of muscular activity in response to the therapist's manipulation of the body provide information about control and the person's ability to surrender it and allow himself to be moved and handled. The type of activity also indicates the person's general way of reacting: those who 'help' the therapist are often helpers in other situations as well.

Tense people expend an unnecessary amount of effort on all their movements. This makes it difficult for them to use muscles or groups of muscles in isolation and to move effectively. We therefore note the capacity for free function in various positions. For example, we test whether:

— the person can move the thigh independently of the back and the pelvis in a sitting position
— the person can stretch the knee in a standing position without involving the pelvis.

Palpation of the muscles

Palpation gives us information about the degree of elasticity or muscular stiffness, the bulk, consistency, and any tenderness or pain. We register these findings for the body as a whole, but with the emphasis on the patient's breathing responses and the plasticity of the muscles. We are also interested in the patient's feelings about being handled and in how he expresses them. In addition to the breathing responses, much can be gathered from motor and autonomic reactions, like facial expression, the expression of the eyes, jerks, motor restlessness, sweating and gooseflesh.

It is generally thought that the greater the degree of muscular stiffness, the greater the tenderness or pain, but experience has shown that the amount of pain is not proportionate to the degree of stiffness. The stiffest muscles are often not tender at all. Pain is primarily linked with changes in tension in the muscles, and tender muscles are often those in which the tension is changing. Muscles that are not at all painful at the beginning of a course of treatment often become tender during the treatment, a sign that the body and the breathing are changing, and we connect this with the altered working conditions of the muscle.

Palpation is not restricted to the problem area, but is always performed on the whole body, in order for the therapist to get an impression of patterns of stress and tensions.

The larynx-jaw-face area is often neglected by physiotherapists.

In psychomotor therapy we are especially interested in it because of its emotional role. The face we present to the world may conceal all kinds of feelings, sometimes behind a stiff mask, with clenched jaws.

Autonomic function

Like other reactions, autonomic reactions must be continually evaluated in context. The degree and type of reaction tell us about the person's way of reacting and about the state of equilibrium of his autonomic system. Pronounced sweating, gooseflesh, and icy hands or feet are examples of disproportionately strong reactions, and indicate that the person reacts to a great extent via the autonomic system.

As well as registering autonomic reactions during the examination, we will understand a good deal through talks and questions. When taking the patient's history, the therapist should go thoroughly into questions of natural functions and disorders connected with autonomically innervated organs.

It is now generally acknowledged that autonomic disorders may be a sign of emotional strain. In such cases we find that we must be careful not to go too far or too fast. The treatment must proceed gradually, in small doses.

Attitude of one's body

Psychomotor therapy should include helping the person to know himself — to become conscious of his body and of the connection between his physical and emotional reaction patterns. Only then can we help him to help himself.

A person who does not realize how he uses, and imposes strain on, himself and his body in everyday life will be unable to change himself. The first step in breaking patterns of tension and bad movement habits is to get to know and trust one's own body. It is equally important for us as therapists to find out about the person's attitude to his body — his body consciousness and awareness. The more we know about this, the better we can meet his needs and make the treatment into something more than a short-term relief from symptoms.

To find out about the patient's proprioception, we ask:

— Do you feel you stand with your knees bent or straight?
— Can you feel that your shoulders are hunched?

To find out about the patient's attitude to and knowledge of the connection between his body and his feelings, we ask:

— What do you do when you are sad? Angry? Happy?

The patient's relationship with his body is also communicated non-verbally all the time, and what he says must be seen in this context i.e:

— Does the patient stare emptily in front of him while the therapist palpates his muscles, yet when asked how he feels about it replies that he is quite relaxed?

The patient's history

Appreciation of the magnitude of the information provided by the body

In psychomotor therapy we place great emphasis on information about the patient's previous illnesses, symptoms, traumas, and what are generally referred to as natural functions. There are several reasons for this.

Previous afflictions and symptoms may recur

Experience has shown that this often happens. The changes that occur during therapy involve not only posture, muscles and breathing, but all the body's organs and functions. When respiratory brakes are released and breath is allowed down into the stomach and pelvic region, afflictions like cystitis may suddenly start to flourish again, and menstrual disturbances or dyspepsia may recur for a while.

When postural changes cause hunched shoulders to sink back to normal, and the back and arms begin to regain their elasticity, the patient often goes through a period with itching of the arms or eczema. This usually happens to people who have had skin problems before.

The patient needs to be told of the possibility of these reactions and that they are part of the treatment process. This is important so that he can accept unpleasant side-effects without anxiety. The taking of drugs or any other form of treatment during such phases should be avoided as far as possible, so as to give the body time and opportunity to adjust naturally and normalize its reactions. An open discussion of past illnesses in connection with the aim and scope of the treatment helps the patient to think in terms of his body's reactions and of the close relation between body and feelings.

Ineffective use of the body due to impairment of reflex innervation

Pain, trauma and operations give rise to reflex muscle contractions that may result in ineffective movement patterns that gradually can become automatic. In psychomotor therapy we therefore ask explicitly about previous operations, plaster casts, etc. and explain why we are asking so as to help the patient into this way of thinking. It is always necessary to include biomechanical and neurophysiological aspects of the body and its movements, but the therapist must take care not to encourage any tendency to somatization on the part of the patient.

Connection between bodily function and emotional and psychological equilibrium

It is important, as we have mentioned before, to ask about natural functions involving autonomic and hormonal factors. Functions like sleeping, appetite, digestion, menstruation and sex life are not traditionally thought of in the context of a person's musculoskeletal problems. And the patient is often reluctant to discuss them with the physiotherapist because he feels they are irrelevant in this situation. We therefore have to help him with explicit questions: Do you get indigestion? How do you sleep? etc.

Information and talks during and after the physical examination

The examination of patients usually starts with the history. In psychomotor therapy the time and the method of recording the patient's history vary.

Whether the patient's history is taken before or after the physical examination, the therapist always asks about and discusses physical reactions and signals during the examination. In other words it is the *body* that is the point of departure for questions and verbal communication. When, for example, we feel during palpation that the patient's feet are cold, we ask him whether he feels the cold, whether he is often cold, and so on. Thus we obtain a general picture of how his body functions, from signals and sense impressions.

It is important to include questions that link feelings with physical reactions:

— What do you feel now? What are you experiencing at this moment?

in situations where the patient's reaction indicates avoidance or evasiveness, e.g. when the patient turns his head away or holds his breath.

Right from the time of the physical examination we generally do our best to get the patient to release his feelings and to see the links between physical and emotional reactions and to think generally in terms of relationships.

The following types of questions can help them to understand this:

— Do you yourself have any ideas about what causes your headaches?
— You say you are overworked. How do you react physically when you experience stress at work?

The importance of the patient's total life situation

We need information about the patient's life in order to understand the relation between his symptoms and the various strains he is exposed to. It is also a help in planning the correct treatment for that particular patient. Since the physical changes are inseparable from psychological ones, this will make demands on the patient's surroundings, and his life must contain alternative possibilities. Psychomotor therapy is not indicated for people in difficult social situations where they are hard pressed and have to pull themselves together to keep on going. The process of psychomotor therapy requires, on the contrary, that the patient is able to heed the signals of his body, to put himself first for a while and to regulate the tempo and amount of his work to suit himself.

Conclusion: comparing and evaluating findings

The conclusions reached after an examination require more than a simple adding up of the findings, because clinical findings are not qualitatively similar, independent units. An evaluation is therefore necessary.

Any isolated finding has little meaning outside the context of the person's whole body and life:

Example A is a person with:

— active, rigid, extended posture
— constricted respiration, constant active expiration, little versatility
— widespread tension
— general stiffness, reduced movability
— little body awareness
— inability to allow manipulation, active resistance to all movements
— body not allowed to be governed by gravity, head and to some extent shoulders held actively but unconsciously in position.

Each of these clinical signs indicates control. Taken together they indicate a very strong physical defence barrier.

All the findings show that he keeps at a distance from his feelings by 'pulling himself together'. The indications are so many, so widespread, so pronounced and so fixed that we can be certain that they are long-term characteristics, part of the personality, and not responses to an acute state of stress.

But how do we interpret findings that give conflicting information?

Example B is a person with:

— flexed posture, slack and deflated
— constricted respiration, constant active expiration, little versatility (Breathing becomes even more restricted in a lying position and when the neck and shoulders are palpated or moved.)
— a lot of slack muscles, i.e. a low degree of muscular stiffness, especially in the legs
— good movability generally
— a certain body awareness
— inability to allow manipulation, active help in all passive movements
— gravity not allowed free rein, head and shoulders held actively in position, of which he is to some extent conscious.

Some of the findings indicate control and some resignation.

Resignation is expressed by the slack, deflated posture and the low degree of stiffness in many muscles. Control is indicated by the breathing and the responses to functional tests, especially in neck and shoulder region.

The distribution is important. He has slack leg muscles and functional control in the neck and shoulder region. Here one can say that control is probably important for this person, in the sense that control of those particular areas helps him to function. If he is deprived of this control he may collapse completely.

A's control of the neck and shoulders and inhibited breathing prevent him from functioning effectively, while B's control of the same areas is a help — he needs it to be able to function at all.

The treatment for these two people will thus be quite different. Although some of the findings are similar when taken in isolation, their implications are quite different when seen in the context of the patient and his life as a whole. Patient B has to be built up before he can allow his defences to give way. If a person is in a difficult situation, he may need to be left in peace. Any treatment in this case would have to be generally stimulating, especially for slack muscles, and encourage body awareness, but not release tension and breathing.

Patient A, on the other hand, needs to relax his defences, although he too needs to be built up. No one can surrender control beyond their emotional capacity. The treatment here would be a cautious and gradual loosening up accompanied by stimulation and training in awareness of the extensors. A direct approach on the muscles and respiration could result in:

— transfer of symptoms and/or a strengthening of physical defences
— a strong emotional reaction.

THE TREATMENT

Aims

The aim of psychomotor therapy is change in the body and its functions. The name suggests that the psychological aspect comes first, which is misleading. We need a name that indicates that the treatment is aimed at the body, and that what actually happens is a complete psychomotor change. The body is the focus of psychomotor therapy, but everything the therapist does is based on an understanding of the body as a psychosocial entity as well as a physical one. As Aadel Bülow-Hansen said: 'We must remember that when anything occurs in the body, something always happens in the mind.'

Treatment sessions

The therapist treats the patient on his own and with no outside disturbances. Each session lasts about an hour. About 45 minutes are spent on working with the body and talking. At the end of the session the patient rests for about ten minutes. This gives him time for reflection and abreaction, for dealing with his feelings and memories. The opportunity of doing this alone contributes to his independence. The last few minutes are used for rounding off the session, to stabilize the patient by making him stand on his own feet in both senses of the term.

A treatment session is highly structured. To achieve a physical and psychological change that is as integrated, stable, and considerate as possible, we aim at a gradual process of development without cathartic outbursts.

Thus, treatment usually takes place once a week, sometimes once every two or three weeks. The treatment may take months or years, depending on how badly afflicted the patient is. The treatment is combined with psychotherapy when necessary.

Exercises and movements

Psychomotor exercises and movements have several goals. The most important is for the breathing to flow freely and spontaneously and to be able to accommodate itself to physical and psychological activity. The following help to achieve this:

— acquiring a functional posture without specific correction
— acquiring body awareness
— acquiring free stretch impulses
— acquiring good flexibility
— promoting stability and equilibrium
— developing the interplay between the whole body, the breathing and the emotions for every movement.

Movements, exercises and massage are continually used to supplement one another. There is no sharp dividing line between examination and treatment, since the patient's reactions to the treatment are the signals according to which the treatment is adjusted.

Functional posture

A special feature of psychomotor therapy is that posture is never specifically corrected, for the following reasons:

— Posture is an expression of an individual's character and personal history. No one can impose a different posture on another person; it would be a violation of their individuality.
— Posture is a product of the balance of tension in the whole body and of the individual's way of breathing, which reflects his way of feeling.

The various flexion and extension patterns are examples of particular types of posture.

The flexed posture is a primitive attitude of safety related to the fetal position. We instinctively adopt it when we feel threatened. An attitude of flexion and adduction becomes a habit in people who develop strong reactions of flight or attack. When a flexion pattern is combined with adduction the person becomes locked, unable to act. A slack flexion pattern indicates a reduced ability to act.

The other main type of posture is extended. Here the person conceals his natural tendency towards flexion and its accompanying emotional signals by *straightening up*, 'pulling himself together', fulfilling his own or others' expectations. With a taut extension pattern we usually find that both the flexion and the extension muscles are rigid (a muscular armour). Like the flexion pattern, the extension pattern may include an abduction, adduction, or slack component.

In traditional physiotherapy a flexed attitude was often corrected by the physiotherapist telling the patient to straighten up. To do this the patient has to induce a tonus in the back muscles that is greater than that in the ventral muscles. He is thus forced into an extension pattern and becomes taut on both sides of the body. People with a flexion pattern often have a considerable amount of respiratory movement in the back, and if the back is straightened and tensed this inhibits their breathing at the back. Since the muscles on the ventral side are short and have to be stretched, the breathing will be inhibited in front as well. Thus patients in such a classical corrected posture often have strained muscles and inhibited breathing. All spontaneity is gone. From the point of view of movement and emotions the patient is in a muscular straightjacket. Unfortunately many physiotherapists and others in similar professions are unaware of the consequences of their specific correction of posture.

In psychomotor therapy we try to promote a spontaneous and autonomous change in posture, and one that is in harmony with the patient's personality and emotional life. When the patient has reached the stage where he himself releases the tension that has been binding him, his body rights itself spontaneously.

To achieve this, we emphasize the 'foundations' of the body, i.e. the legs and feet, at the beginning of the treatment. Unless the axis, flexibility and stability of the body's supports are in good condition, there is little point in changing the upper parts. Thus we work especially thoroughly with the feet and legs. The synergy between the quadriceps, the dorsal flexors of the ankle, and the proximal joints of the toes is particularly important, since it provides good stability in a standing position. Changes in axis, e.g. in the spinal column or the position of the head, shift the centre of gravity. To compensate for such changes, we work upwards and downwards all the time. All changes, wherever they occur, require a general reorganization. When we work on the longitudinal axes we combine this with work on breathing and on the stretch impulses triggered by yawning. Emotionally speaking it is important to help the patient 'stand on his own feet' in both senses of the term before beginning on the more emotionally-charged areas of the upper body.

Body awareness

Work on body awareness is an integral part of everything we do in psychomotor therapy. Body awareness implies that the patient is conscious of the functions of his body and is able to accept the feelings involved. During this process the patient often becomes more aware that his body is himself: a self that feels and functions. The process strengthens the ego so that it is able to be outgoing or reserved according to the demands of complex social situations.

It is particularly important to obtain consciousness of the extensor muscles in the inner range of movement at an early stage, since tense people often have poor consciousness of these muscles. Working on consciousness of the extensors causes the flexors, which are often short in these cases, to relax.

Stretching exercises open the way for free breathing, yawning and feelings. For example, when a person with open respiratory organs stretches out his arm the movement of inspiration will increase on that side of the thorax. A complete yawn requires free movement of the thorax. Inhibited respiration checks the expression of feelings. As the inhibition lessens, the feelings rise to the surface. The yawn is a barometer for measuring the blocks in the body and is a good indicator of the patient's progress. It is also a therapeutic aid; we use it deliberately to release muscular and respiratory brakes.

We make conscious use of the connection between respiration, muscles and yawning. This can be done in several ways. While we loosen up the flexors of the arms and carry out stretching movements, we ask the patient to wriggle his fingers and move his jaw. This adjusts the body so that yawning, or elements of it, is spontaneously triggered. Yawning can only take place if a certain level of musculorespiratory relaxation has been achieved. Thus we promote free stretching in the body, and thereby looseness and flexibility — the most important hallmarks of good body function, which depend on the minimum of muscular and respiratory inhibitions.

Flexibility

Flexibility exercises are especially important for promoting suppleness, relaxation and versatility in the body. They consist of active and passive movements, rocking and small movements, especially small rotating movements, with the body in a number of different positions. These exercises relax and lengthen short muscles. They also foster the patient's ability to surrender to the force of gravity, i.e. to remain passive, not to help or resist when the therapist moves part of his body. With the active movements we aim at the least possible use of the muscles, and cooperation between muscular work and the force of gravity.

The psychological aspect of these exercises is that the patient is able to surrender control of a situation. In the passive exercises this involves trusting other people, in this case the therapist, and in the active ones it involves relying on oneself.

Stability and equilibrium

Stability and equilibrium are a result of complex processes. When a patient has undergone a considerable amount of physical and psychological adjustment during a session, he needs to experience physical stability and balance to counteract excessive emotional arousal and to re-establish and develop an emotional equilibrium. We make a point of this by having the patient stand and sum up his impressions of his body at the end of a session and give way to any stretching impulses. One of the most important exercises in psychomotor therapy is often used to further stability and balance. The patient stands with his feet parallel and apart at the width of the hips. The knees are slightly flexed and the back is bent forwards so that the arms hang down over the feet. Ideally the fingertips now point to the navicular. After the therapist has carried out small movements of segments of the upper half of the body, the patient bends and stretches his knees with an undulating movement that runs right through the body. The rocking movement in the knees rhythmically stimulates the proprioceptors in the forefeet, which facilitates stretching impulses. When the patient pulls upright from this bent position, his balance and stability are often noticeably altered. People often say things like: 'I can't remember when I was last able to stand so well'.

Physical interaction exercises

All the exercises have an element of interaction, but some contain more than others. In one such exercise the patient concentrates on gentle movements with his tongue and jaws while relaxing and letting his breath flow freely (without force or control). If he then gently wriggles his fingers or toes, this may trigger a stretching movement that develops into a full yawn. This is like a child's automatic yawn when it rubs its eyes. These bodily interactions are sometimes very primitive and may make the patient aware of himself as a whole. Sometimes memories from the time these functions were suppressed rise to the surface. The awareness aided by the yawn often brings further insight. One patient said: 'I feel that I can see and hear more distinctly than before, not only sounds and colours, but also the feelings attached to them. I feel I have become psychic'.

Massage and grips

Psychomotor massage is based on classical Scandinavian massage, but the principal difference lies in the relation between grip and breathing. Breathing is an essential part of the response to massage, and some grips are adapted so as to moderate respiration, while others facilitate inspiration, and others again help the patient let his breath go, or sigh. We stimulate the spread of the movement of inspiration by pulling and pressing lightly at the ribs. Pressure on the chest is also used to promote thorough expiration, which in turn often leads to spontaneous deep inspiration.

In psychomotor therapy we pinch tender muscles as a way of bringing about respiratory and emotional changes. If the person holds his breath or forces his breathing, he cannot release his tension, but if he sighs, for example, this reduces the inner pressure and loosens the inner control mechanisms that maintain emotional and motor defence habits.

'Letting one's breath go' can be combined with an emotional discharge proportionate to the discomfort of the pinch. We usually tell the patient to let out an 'Ow!' or an 'Aah!' or similar exclamations, but the point is that the outburst must not be mechanical; it should be a genuine emotional response to the experience.

Some people are so inhibited that they cannot produce such reactions by themselves. We ask them to try sighing, shaking us off, or kicking. For many of them the most difficult response is to cry 'Ow!', and for some it helps to whisper the word at first, then to say it, and finally to put feeling into it.

We encourage the patient to express his pain in any way he chooses except by holding his breath, biting back the pain, or accepting it. The following are the sort of reactions we encourage to a pinch in the triceps surae:

— The patient gasps, i.e. takes a deep inspiration culminating in a passive relaxed expiration.
— The patient pulls his leg away from the pain and gasps at the same time.

The important point here is that he goes 'out to meet' the pain, sets a limit on it.

— The patient gives an exclamation, usually 'Ow!', at the same time letting out his breath. When he kicks stretching impulses are triggered, and the respiratory, motor and verbal expressions form a unit.

The importance of this procedure is that whatever else the patient does, he releases his breath and his tension.

A conscious use of a painful pinch or pressure on the muscle is an effective way of promoting spontaneous changes in breathing; at the same time it helps the person out of old undesirable habits in tackling difficult situations. Because the pain is so slight, really only an unpleasant sensation, the person is able to go out to meet it; in other words to kick, stretch out, and/or set his own limits verbally. This means that he responds to a situation by mastering it and not by flight or withdrawal.

In this way the patient learns new ways of coping with difficulties or unpleasantnesses. When he lets go of his breathing he lets out accumulated tension, and the unpleasantness does not remain inside him. By learning to project himself, muscularly and verbally, in a structured way, he also learns to set limits on himself. This can be used in other situations in life as well. Thus the interplay between feelings, breathing and physical expression in a psychomotor session helps to change posture, movements and motor and emotional habits generally.

Between the 'painful' stimuli, the therapist uses larger, stroking movements to help the patient calm down. These larger movements also help the patient to define the limits of his body and thus, by giving him an impression of his body as a whole, they increase his self-awareness.

Attitudes to feeling in psychomotor therapy

A physiotherapist used to be thought of as a sort of Wailing Wall. She was supposed to refer the patient to a physician if he began to discuss his problems or reacted emotionally during the treatment. This has changed. As emotional reactions are an integrated part of the changes of the body, it is rather antitherapeutic not to let the patient react emotionally in other ways than through the body. More than in other parts of physiotherapy the psychomotor therapy raises questions like:

— The type and extent of conflicts and feelings that can or should be allowed in the treatment

— The point at which a specialist in psychotherapy should be called in.

In psychomotor therapy contact with the patient is obtained via the body; listening and talking are secondary. Most people find this a very satisfactory approach. The therapist does not ask personal questions unless absolutely necessary, but when a secure relationship has been established between patient and therapist the former usually begins to talk about himself quite spontaneously, about his problems, conflicts, and anything else he feels able to bring up. The therapist's position vis-á-vis the patient is that of a fellow being who is willing to listen. Being able to put his thoughts and associations into words helps the patient to clarify his ideas and his attitudes to the conflicts, and being able to laugh and cry or mourn together with another person gives a feeling of relief and liberation.

However, the therapist should be more than a listener. It is her responsibility to help the patient gain insight into his symptoms and his particular way of reacting. Helping the patient to see the connection between his symptoms and his life situation has become a natural and integrated part of the treatment. If the patient suffers from tension headaches or migraine, the therapist may ask: 'Have you noticed any situations or factors that influence your headaches?' Or she may suggest that he notes down exactly what happens before he gets a headache, perhaps something he disliked or was afraid of? The next step is to get him to *feel* what he does with his breathing and his body in difficult situations. A great deal of insight can be gained by this.

The younger generation of psychomotor therapists have carried this method a step further. They try to help the patient to a greater perception of his own feelings both during and between sessions.

The type of conflict, and the extent to which a conflict should be acted out during treatment, depend on the therapist's own development and maturity, and on the possibilities for supervision and cooperation she has otherwise.

Recourse to psychotherapy becomes necessary when the patient's feelings and conflicts begin to interfere with his daily life. Very often the patient himself brings up the question of psychotherapy. Psychomotor therapy helps a person to become conscious of his feelings and conflicts and it may promote a gradual maturing of the personality, so that those who need psychotherapy eventually come to accept that they do.

TRAINING IN PSYCHOMOTOR THERAPY

Psychomotor therapy is a specialized training carried out under the auspices of the Norwegian Physical Therapy Association. It takes four years of part-time work, and is deliberately staggered over such a long period to ensure that knowledge, insight and clinical judgement are thoroughly integrated in the students, and to give their personalities time to develop along these lines. Clinical work is an essential part of the training.

After having finished education from a Physical Therapy College, the training consists of a basic course of general knowledge and an advanced course on the psychomotor approach. The basic course, which lasts about two years part-time, is an introduction to the fundamental interaction between psyche and soma. The objective is to give the students the necessary foundation for carrying out a complete physical examination and trains them to distinguish broadly between symptoms with primarily mechanical causes and those with psychosocial causes. It also teaches a number of basic methods for use in individual and group therapy.

After the basic course comes the actual psychomotor method and approach, which also lasts about two years part-time. After an introductory course the student begins with her own patients under supervision. She herself also undergoes psychomotor therapy. This is essential so that she can understand and experience the physical and psychological processes the therapy sets in motion. During this period the students are taught both individually and in large and small groups. During the last six months the student writes an independent paper on a subject of her choice connected with psychomotor therapy.

PSYCHOMOTOR THERAPY AS A SOURCE OF INSPIRATION

Psychomotor therapy has had a generally strong creative effect on Norwegian physiotherapy. It has also enriched it by systematic surveys and research carried out by psychomotor therapists in areas connected with an understanding of the body as a whole (Sundsvold & Vaglum, 1985). This research has also contributed to psychiatric diagnostic theory, and has led to the development of physiotherapeutic approaches in psychiatry. Various 'schools' and methods have developed within the psychomotor tradition, but its most important contribution has been that its way of thinking and methods of treatment have influenced Norwegian physiotherapy generally. It counterbalances the fragmented view of human beings and their bodies that dominates Western medicine, and helps to compensate for sectorization and narrow specialization.

REFERENCES

Braatøy T 1947 De nervøse sinn. Cappelen Forlag, Oslo
Braatøy T 1954 Fundamentals of psychoanalytic technique. John Wiley, New York
Bunkan B H 1985 Muskelspenninger og kroppsbilde. Universitetsforlaget, Oslo
Bunkan B H, Thornquist E, Radøy L 1982 Psykomotorisk behandling. Festskrift til Aadel Bülow-Hansen. Universitetsforlaget, Oslo
Christiansen B 1972 Thus speaks the body, 2nd edn. Arno Press, New York
Johnsen L 1975 Integrert respirasjonsterapi. Universitetsforlaget, Oslo
Øvreberg G, Andersen T 1986 Aadel Bülow-Hansens fysioterapi, Norway
Sundsvold M Ø, Vaglum P 1985 Muscular pains and psychopathology, evaluation by GRM method. In: Hoskins Michel T (ed) Pain. Churchill Livingstone, London
Thornquist E 1983 Lungefysioterapi. Universitetsforlaget, Oslo
Thornquist E, Bunkan B H 1986 Hva er psykomotorisk behandling. Universitetsforlaget, Oslo

4. Physiotherapy as an approach in psychiatric care with emphasis on Body Awareness Therapy

G. Roxendal

BACKGROUND

During the last few decades there has been a move towards a complete change in psychiatric care in Sweden as in other industrialized countries. The big mental hospitals, often with more than 1000 patients, are being reduced and care is being decentralised into smaller units with open care psychiatric teams and smaller hospitals. Traditional psychiatric care, dominated by nursing mentally ill patients, is changing to treatment and rehabilitation aimed towards a normal social life outside the hospital. Existing institutions are seldom suitable for this new purpose, which leads to a sometimes difficult process of change for mental health workers. Mental disorders are commonly associated with motor disturbances. They may be a part of the disease, a side-effect of treatment with neuroleptics, a result of institutionalized care or a combination of these elements. Hospitalized psychiatric care has by tradition been directed more towards symptom reduction than evaluating and treating possible causes of the symptoms. The treatment methods have mainly been pharmacological and verbal therapeutic approaches. The interest in treatment methods which work directly with motor disturbances is now increasing. These methods are seen as supplements to the traditional treatment of mental disorders.

Traditional physiotherapy in psychiatric care has provided treatment for physical disorders using traditional somatic physiotherapy methods. In addition, the need for physical activity for the mentally disabled has been realized since Greek and Roman times. Such activities were again put into use and developed further during the 1940s and 1950s.

Wilhelm Reich (1945) has described the increasing connection between psychic trauma, muscular tension and the stress of everyday life, especially in Western, industrialized countries. This has resulted in a focus on muscular hypo- and hypertension and its relation to symptoms and altered motor function in various groups of patients, especially those with neurotic symptoms and psychiatric illness. Several techniques for muscular relaxation have been developed, such as Jacobson's Progressive Relaxation (1948) and Schultz' Autogenic Training (1960). In Sweden, psychiatric physiotherapy has included these three elements: traditional somatic physiotherapy, physical activities and muscular relaxation. In modern psychiatric care, however, the need for therapeutic methods working with motor function as an expression of a person's inner life has been obvious.

Current development

Since the 1970s a new approach has been developing, with exercises for body perception and body experiencce being used in psychiatric physiotherapy. The motor functions are mostly trained in total coordination patterns where the movement itself is combined with elements of non-verbal experience and expression. A newly developed treatment method in Swedish psychiatric physiotherapy is Body Awareness Therapy which is described below.

PSYCHIATRIC PHYSIOTHERAPY IN PHYSIOTHERAPY EDUCATION

In Sweden the share of psychiatric theory and treatment methods in physiotherapy training increased markedly in 1978. In 1983 basic physiotherapy education was changed into a common university training for physiotherapists and occupational therapists, the Rehabilitation Postgraduate Course, with separate professional courses. These changes have included an increased amount of time being spent on psychosomatic and psychiatric studies, including theory and practice.

For trained physiotherapists the National University Office has decided to arrange an advanced training with separate courses, including one for psychiatric physiotherapy. This university course is aimed towards in-depth professional training.

PSYCHIATRIC PHYSIOTHERAPY

Patients

Different groups of patients may benefit from psychiatric physiotherapy. These groups are sometimes organized according to diagnosis such as schizophrenia or anorexia nervosa. Generally it is more practical to group patients according to their place in general psychiatric care and their need for treatment. Physiotherapists often meet their patients grouped in the following way:

— psychogeriatric patients, mostly in hospital care
— patients in long-term hospital care, mainly suffering from brain damage after toxicomania and psychotic disorders, in particular schizophrenia
— patients in short-term hospital care, with different kinds of psychoses, borderline, anorexia nervosa, different kinds of neuroses
— patients in open care and day wards with all kinds of diagnostic groups including after-care in long-term treatment programmes
— psychosomatic disorders in psychiatric and somatic care
— vocational rehabilitation in psychiatric care with multiple diagnoses, mostly in after-care.

Goal of therapy

The general goal of treatment in psychiatric care, to cure mental illness, to decrease suffering or to increase the patient's level of function, is of course also shared by physiotherapists.

Different health workers contribute to this general goal with their specific professional knowledge and experience. The principal physiotherapeutic goal is to help the patient integrate the body in his total experience of identity. This will be further explained in the description of treatment methods below.

The specific goal of psychiatric physiotherapy is dependent on the time available. For short-term treatment, symptom reduction may be the main goal. A long-term objective might be an increased level of function and satisfaction of life.

Reduction of symptoms as a goal

Whether reduction of symptoms is a short-term goal of therapy or not depends upon the type of symptoms and what the symptoms represent in the disease process. Some examples of different kinds of symptoms are:

— Physical dysfunction or pain which has not markedly altered the personality structure. Examples of such symptoms are reduced mobility after fracture and temporary headache due to stress. Relief of such symptoms will increase the patient's self-esteem and improve his social function. Reduction of these symptoms is a basic objective for psychiatric physiotherapy.
— Psychotic symptoms which have a disintegrating effect on consciousness, e.g. disturbed body image boundaries in schizophrenic patients. These symptoms can be expressed, for example, in a patient's searching for his head which 'has vanished', or in the anxiety caused by a feeling of disintegrating body image boundaries. Reduction of these symptoms is also a basic objective of psychiatric physiotherapy.
— Vague bodily symptoms such as pain or tension as an expression of deep personal or psychological disturbances. Increased body consciousness gained in body-centered therapy can temporarily aggravate symptoms of this kind. In the long run, however, it can lead to a growing understanding of the connection between the patient's life situation and the symptoms. In this case, the patient has to choose between taking steps to decrease the symptom (maybe also change his life style) and going on living with the symptom. A short-term reduction of such symptoms is not always a self-evident goal of the treatment.
— Symptoms that are elements of the defence system against agony. Relief of such symptoms might trigger the agony and is not a self-evident short-term goal of treatment.

INVESTIGATIONS AND TREATMENT PLANNING

To be able to assess the treatment, the patient's problem should be analysed. If there is more than one problem, the physiotherapist and patient should choose one problem to work with where results are sufficiently realistic to be attainable. The resources should also be analysed: the patient's resources expressed in terms of body experience and motor abilities. Finally the patient's motivation should be analysed, his goals and his general level of activity which will affect his ability to reach his goals.

The choice of treatment methods in psychiatric care naturally requires special information about the patient. Four different kinds of information can be collected:

1. The patient's subjective (self) report
2. Projective tests
3. The physiotherapist's observations
4. Special evaluation of the particular dysfunction and/or the patient's bodily resources.

The patient's self-report

Written self-reports

Several systems have been developed to get the patient's opinion about his state. He can answer rather structured questions such as 'Have you got a headache?', 'Do you feel tension in the muscles in your neck, shoulders, low back?' on written self-report sheets. Or the questions can be semi-structured such as 'Have you got aches or pains? Where?'

The patient can be asked to mark on a drawn human figure where he feels his pain. It is also possible to put open questions on the written self-report, such as 'What is the dominating pain? Please describe it.'

The written self-report can be filled in independently by the patient, or the physiotherapist can guide the answering during an interview.

Visual analogous scales (VAS)

Many variations of visual analogous scales or semantic differential scales have been constructed. This is a continuum with definitions of specific states at each end, e.g. 'I feel quite well, couldn't feel better' at one end and 'I feel terrible, couldn't be worse' at the other. The patient puts a mark for his actual state of well-being on the line. Afterwards the physiotherapist measures and quantifies the patient's rating.

Interviews

The self-report may also be given verbally in more or less structured interviews. When interviewing for symptoms or dysfunctions it may be suitable to use general rules throughout the enquiry. Every symptom should be answered in concrete terms on the following aspects before continuing to the next question:

— Frequency (How often?)
— Duration (How long-standing?)
— Intensity (Quality of the symptom. Which functions in daily life are inhibited by the symptom?)
— Ability to master (Does the patient master the situation by himself or does he need help from others?)

The physiotherapist is taught to conduct the interview calmly and with a therapeutic attitude.

Projective tests

A projective test includes obtaining a picture or reaction from the patient which is interpreted by the assessor. Draw-a-person, draw-a-house, describe what images you can see in inkblots are examples of tasks for patients in projective tests. Seymor Fisher and others have studied patients' body image boundaries with the Penetration and Barrier Score, that is interpretations of reactions on inkblots (Fisher & Cleveland, 1958).

To use projective tests the assessor should have had a basic education in psychology or psychiatry *and* undergone a special training to interpret the results. The reliability of projective tests has until now not been satisfactorily shown. Projective tests are rarely used by physiotherapists in Sweden.

The physiotherapist's observations

Observations are a very important part of all physiotherapeutic evaluations. In psychiatric care, observations concern the patient's motor behaviour as a whole, including posture, gait, non-verbal expression, if and how the patient has eye-contact during an interview, sweating hands, sighing, breathing, etc. The observations can be structured according to specific needs and they should always be related to the patient's self-report.

Taking photographs, films or videos can be very useful 'preserved' observations. These photographs and films are in some cases useful in therapy, especially when treating eating disorders. The patients often perceive their mirror image quite differently from the images seen in photographs. It is, however, necessary to follow ethical rules when using photographs. One way to handle this problem is to use instamatic cameras and let patients take care of their own photographs.

Special physiotherapeutic evaluations

Often a general examination and assessment of the patient's main complaints need to be completed. These investigations are the same as those taught and used in somatic physiotherapy. Examination techniques of muscular tension and posture developed in Norway and described by Heir-Bunkan (1979) and Ostbye-Sundsvold (1975) are also widely used in Sweden.

The Body Awareness Scale (BAS)

There is a scale in use by physiotherapists in psychiatric care called the Body Awareness Scale (BAS) (Roxendal, 1985). This is a rating scale where the assessor rates symptoms and behaviour from the healthy to the most extreme degree of symptom or dysfunction. BAS is constructed with the psychiatric rating scale as a model. It has 16 items for the patient's reported information, 10 from a psychiatric symptom scale (CPRS, Comprehensive Psychopathological Rating Scale) (Aasberg et al, 1978) and 6 newly constructed items. It also has 31 items for observed information, 13 from the CPRS and 18 newly constructed body items.

In the beginning the BAS may seem extensive for clinical use. A factor analysis has been computed for data reduction and has grouped the 47 items in easy-to-understand factors. The BAS has been statistically tested and found to be reliable and valid for clinical use (Roxendal, 1985).

The BAS is a new type of measuring instrument since:

— it collects a combination of psychiatric and
  physiotherapeutic data
— the physiotherapeutic information is an attempt to include

aspects on motor ability as well as emotional expression in the patient's motor behaviour
— rating with the BAS includes a structured interview which concerns aspects of the patient's body experience and attitudes to his body.

TREATMENT METHODS

This section contains an overview of treatment methods used by physiotherapists in psychiatric care. The methodological core of psychiatric physiotherapy in Sweden is Body Awareness Therapy (BAT) (Roxendal, 1981, 1985) which will be described separately.

Body Awareness Therapy (BAT)

Background

The theoretical basis of Body Awareness Therapy is the theory of motor ability and motor dysfunctions taught in physiotherapy schools.

In practice, Body Awareness Therapy differs from traditional physiotherapy in that it stimulates sensory awareness and uses it on a conscious level in training. Exercises in Body Awareness Therapy are directed towards body management as a whole including body consciousness and motor functions and not towards a local dysfunction or pain.

Treatment of motor functions given with a sufficient degree of sensory activation often triggers emotional reactions. This is consciously used in Body Awareness Therapy, which is thus based on a biological foundation in combination with psychotherapeutic means.

Body Awareness Therapy is based on the assumption that each voluntary human movement contains emotional meaning (Piret & Beziers, 1979). Each physical activity has several psychological components, e.g. the purpose of the movement, the movement as an expression of the person's inner life and the person's psychological experience of the movement.

Indications

Body Awareness Therapy is intended for treatment of diseases where disturbances in body consciousness and motor behaviour are an important part of the pathological picture. It can be used in psychotic states with disturbed body consciousness, body image and psychomotor behaviour as well as neurotic states with depreciation of the body or appearance or disturbances of body management. It is also used for psychosomatic disorders. For schizophrenic patients, Body Awareness Therapy can be combined with drug treatment, social training and psychotherapy.

Goal of therapy

The general goal for psychiatric physiotherapy, to integrate the body in the patient's total experience of identity, contains improved body awareness and decreased psychomotor dysfunctions.

In Body Awareness Therapy this general goal is divided into different aspects of a person's relationship with his body:

1. Increased experience and consciousness of the body in general, including perception and knowledge of the body
2. Improved management of the body — motor ability — in everyday life
3. Re-establishment of a disturbed body-image (the psychic representation of the body and its parts)
4. Relief of symptoms related to poor use of the body
5. Increased consciousness of the movement pattern, the 'personal style' in posture, movement and behaviour
6. Increased motivation for movement and exercises
7. Improved non-verbal communication.

Two complementary aspects in Body Awareness Therapy

Body Awareness Therapy in practice is based upon two complementary aspects of people's body experience and movement pattern.

The first aspect concerns *general movement functions*, such as posture, gait, breathing and movements of daily living. The second aspect deals with the person's *unique individuality* in terms of body experience and movement pattern. These two aspects require different orientations of technique, Basic and Expressive Body Awareness Therapy, which will be described separately. In the clinic, however, these two techniques are used in the same therapeutic setting. In both techniques the patient's sensory awareness is stimulated and used as a therapeutic tool. Perception exercises are included and time is allowed for the patient to react and talk about his experience in both techniques.

Basic Body Awareness Therapy: general movement functions

The main source of information for basic Body Awareness Therapy is Jacques Dropsy through his courses in Tai chi chuan and his books *Vivre Dans Son Corps* (1973) and *Le Corps Bien Accordé* (1984).

Therapeutic philosophy

In Basic Body Awareness Therapy, the patient is being trained to do special exercises under the physiotherapist's guidance. The role of the physiotherapist is more educative than psychotherapeutic. The therapeutic process can be compared with supportive psychotherapy: bodily ego forces are built up. The physiotherapist does not invite the release of defence mechanisms against conflicts or emotional outbursts, but some bodily defences can be weakened and strong feelings can be set free. The non-verbal therapeutic process is supported verbally by short talks. The purpose of these talks is partly to introduce the patient to verbal psychotherapy, working with the reactions in Body Awareness Therapy, and partly to give him insight into the psycho-physical functions being trained. The non-verbal intervention may prepare the patient for a continued verbal phase of treatment (May et al, 1963).

Specialized techniques

The basic technique consists of structured exercises directed partly towards body management as a whole and partly towards particular elements of this management. The following is a brief description of these elements.

1. The relation to the ground is considered to be an important part of motor function and behaviour. Every movement has its starting point. Safe contact with the floor is necessary for efficient movements and coordination, e.g. body-posture, gait and movements of the trunk. The vertical flow of energy, described by

Reich among others (with horizontal inhibitions at different levels), requires relaxed and safe contact with the ground. One might also speculate about a person's physical relation to the ground as an expression of his mental stability or emotional security.

The patient's relation to the ground is trained by directing his attention to his contact with the floor and his experience of the weight of his body in different positions. Exercises related to gravity, e.g. heel-raising and knee-bending, improve the patient's relation to the ground in action; see Figures 4.1 and 4.2.

2. The centre-line of the body. The body posture and balance in the upright position are described in terms of arranging the parts of the body along the centre-line of the body. Deviations from this centre-line cause postural problems with increased muscular tension and these can develop into disturbed balance. Activated postural muscles require little physical energy (Carlsö,

Fig. 4.1 Heel raising

Fig. 4.2 Knee bending

1968; Piret & Beziers, 1979). With proper coordination, standing does not tire the body.

Exercises aimed at improving body posture start from the position of the feet. The body posture is dynamic, and later on it is therefore trained to be integrated with movements and breathing.

3. The movement centre. The human body can be seen as a combination of two functional systems: the lower one with the feet, legs and pelvis; and the upper one with the chest, arms and head. The two systems are connected in the movement centre of the body, between the navel and the breastbone, and with the abdominal obliques and the diaphragm as the most important muscles (Dropsy, 1973, 1984). See also Figure 4.3 (Roxendal, 1985).

The patients train to initiate movements from the movement centre; see, for example, Figures 4.4 and 4.5 for the pair of movements, contract and expand (stretch). They also train to integrate movement coordination and breathing, which is described below.

4. Breathing adapts to body movements and changes in the amount of activity undertaken. It becomes blocked or stimulated

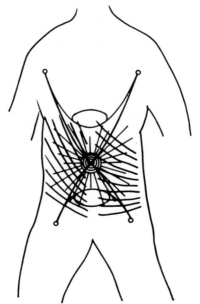

Fig. 4.3 The movement centre

Fig. 4.4   Contract exercise

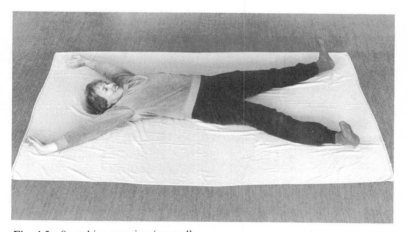

Fig. 4.5   Stretching exercise, 'expand'

by different emotions and feelings. Psychic trauma or disease often creates lasting disturbances in breathing.

Breathing exercises are frequently introduced by directing the patient's attention to 'how his breathing works all by itself'. In other exercises the patient is told to emit sound on exhaling and integrate his breathing with movements.

Exercises with breathing and the voice easily arouse emotional reactions. They must therefore be introduced with great care and professionalism.

5. *The boundaries of the body* are briefly defined as the individual's experience of his limits towards his surroundings. In Body Awareness Therapy the boundaries of the body are seen as one component in a total experience of identity. According to clinical experience, patients with acute psychosis often express agony in connection with disturbances in the body boundaries. The patient may say that he is outside his body, or that horns are growing out of his forehead.

The patients' acceptance of physical contact with objects or people around them may be seen as an aspect of body boundaries. This acceptance varies with different states of mental disorders. Some patients have kept their fists clenched for a long time in order to avoid touching things or people. Exaggerated need of closeness and contact also occurs but is not often expressed.

In Body Awareness Therapy patients repeatedly experience their physical limits within their surroundings, e.g. by turning and rolling on the floor. Holding hands in formal dances and games is an example of a further step in this treatment. The exercises are never allowed to threaten the defence system created by some patients to protect their body boundaries.

6. *Muscular tension and relaxation.* Muscular tension is often part of a complex problem. People with hypertension in certain muscle groups, who are incapable of relaxing these muscles, frequently have a low tension in other muscles. A connection between muscular tension and emotional conflicts has also been described (Alexander, 1932; Bunkan-Heir, 1979; Jacobson, 1948; Lowen, 1971). The state of muscular tension is here seen as part of the total dimension of controlling muscular activity. This dimension includes the ability to exert the muscles, to relax them, and to alternate between these two levels of activity. Muscular tension should also be adapted to different kinds of daily activity.

Specialized relaxation techniques are not part of Body Awareness Therapy. Yet harmonized muscular tension is usually achieved in the treatment.

7. *Energy and direction: two important elements in body movements.* When exercising, the patient's attention is directed towards different elements of body movements, including energy and direction. The energy for the movements is taken from the floor, through the legs and central muscles — those for posture and breathing. These muscles have great endurance and are not easily exhausted (Carlsö, 1968; Dropsy, 1973, 1984; Lowen, 1971). Peripheral muscles, which have less staying power, are used in the exercises to give direction to the movements; this element of movement does not require much energy. With such central coordination it is possible for the movements to become harmonious and relaxed. Even concentrated exercise should not tire the body but make the patient feel vitalized.

Expressive, individualistic-oriented Body Awareness Therapy

Therapeutic philosophy

The exercises in the expressive technique are less structured than those in the basic one. The emphasis is placed on personal style, as expressed in posture, gait and associated movements. In the expressive technique, the patient obtains self-experience with different patterns of motor behaviour. Exercises involving interaction between pairs or groups of patients are also included. In the interaction exercises, the patients can observe others' reactions to their own behaviour and are made conscious of their own reactions to others' behaviour in a sheltered situation. As tools in a total approach to body awareness, different components of motor behaviour are observed and trained, such as gait, rhythm, voice, relation to one's mirror image and interaction between members in the group.

In Expressive Body Awareness Therapy, the physiotherapist is less active and less guiding than in the basic technique. There is also more room for the patient to take responsibility and show initiative. The physiotherapist carefully observes the patients' reactions in order to let the patients' needs and initiatives direct the therapy. In the expressive technique, the patient frequently reacts emotionally and old memories are revived; this makes verbalizing necessary. In groups of in-patients, staff from the ward take part, mostly psychotherapists or group leaders. This enables them to continue the therapy verbally in another therapeutic setting.

Specialized techniques

1. The gait. As a mechanical function, gait is largely the same in different individuals. However, the movement pattern differs markedly between adult individuals; it is unique and personal, comparable to posture and voice. In prolonged walking exercises, the patients' attention is directed towards the perception of their gait and towards different ways of walking. Variations in gait can:

— relate to time — slowly, slower, quickly, quicker
— relate to space — around the edges of the room, to the middle of the room, in a circle, in a figure of eight, in straight lines, in curved lines
— relate to directions — forwards, backwards, sideways
— be coordinated in different ways — on the toes, on the heels, with the knees bent, with the shoulders raised, with the arms still, with big steps, with small steps, with a stamp, as silently as possible
— be coordinated with the behaviour of someone in the group
— with hands in the pockets, with crossed arms, with feet turned inwards, with feet turned outwards.

After every change in the coordination of the gait, the patients are told to walk 'as usual'. This helps the members of the group to become familiar with their own gait. Gait is also trained through individuals' meeting each other and in groups, when patients can observe different movement patterns performed by others. It gives them the chance to become aware of and react to individual traits in non-verbal behaviour.

2. Rhythm. The life and movements of human beings are subject to constant rhythmical changes, as are those of other beings. Physiologically dominated rhythms involve heart beats, breathing and the menstrual cycle, where the connection with psychic life is evident. Every individual is considered to have his own basic rhythm which varies in different life situations. This personal basic rhythm adjusts to other external rhythms. Studies in industry have shown that it is easier to adjust to a faster than to a slower rhythm than one's own.

A sense of rhythm is trained in different ways. One way is to start from a personal rhythm, such as breathing, by merely observing it. The breathing can then form the rhythmical basis for simple exercises. Rhythms are also trained without reference to breathing. In a later stage patients lead each other in rhythmical improvisations.

3. The human voice is just as personal as posture and gait. Physiologically, it depends on breathing, the inner speech muscles, and the muscles of the jaws and the lips. The voice also discloses moods and emotions. Many patients become embarrassed when they hear their own voice, especially those who lack self-confidence.

Voice exercises often start with the therapist asking the patient to emit sounds on exhaling. A combination of movements and sound, sometimes reminiscent of old work songs, trains the patient to integrate his breathing and voice with his body and movements. Through shared recitations of simple texts, patients become accustomed to listening to their voices and to practising using them. Repeated presentation, where each member of the group states his or her name which is then repeated by the others, is training both for the voice and for the experience of identity. Many of these exercises are pleasurable and improve the atmosphere in the group.

Exercises with the voice are performed very carefully, since they easily arouse emotional reactions.

4. Relation to one's mirror image. The reservation that many people have towards their own mirror image can, in psychiatric patients, mean that they do not accept their appearance and body. These patients avoid the mirror except for necessary checks of appearance and dress.

Body Awareness Therapy is performed in a gym with a wall mirror, not in order to correct a patient's posture or performance of the exercises but as a tool for identification. In the beginning, many patients cannot move in front of the mirror; the physiotherapist then turns the group in another direction. The patients continue to train in a room with a mirror. After a while the exercises can be performed facing the mirror. This gives practical training in the habit of seeing and looking at one's mirror image. The aim is to accept one's appearance as a part of one's identity.

5. In interaction exercises, the patients test their non-verbal behaviour in meeting and cooperating with each other. They also have the opportunity to practise the skills and movement patterns they have acquired in their personal training. There is some interaction in every group therapy session. It can occur spontaneously during the meeting exercises, or the physiotherapist may introduce different kinds of interaction exercises such as presentation, movement interaction with a partner or in groups, or games.

In presentation exercises, the patients learn to say their names, hear their names mentioned by other people, listen to and remember other people's names and turn to other people and tell them their names. The presentation exercises continue even when all members of the group know each other's names. A presentation may also be performed non-verbally, in movement or gesture. The exercise often includes an answer — a respondent or the whole group repeats the name or the movement once or several times.

Meetings. There are many variations of 'meeting' exercises where people come into contact with each other. One is to try to avoid eye-contact; or the patients try to look at each other secretly — they try to see without being seen; or they greet one another. The meeting exercises are also combined with other exercises such as a certain body posture, a movement or a presentation.

In the partner exercises, different aspects of interaction can be emphasized, such as cooperation, confidence, or energy release in games or in combat. The terms 'contact exercises' and 'security exercises' are avoided in Body Awareness Therapy, as is release of aggression. The physiotherapist gives the patients the opportunity to explore their need for contact, how secure or insecure they feel, and whether they are charged with surplus energy that they need to act out. Acting out energy can occur spontaneously; a cooperation exercise can turn into a combat game between partners or groups. The physiotherapist may also suggest formal combat games when somebody expresses a need to release energy or a surplus of energy.

Interaction exercises in groups. Non-verbal interaction exercises can provide good opportunities for training concentration and social contact. Games and dances from different countries are a natural part of Body Awareness Therapy. Coordination and rhythm are trained simultaneously with the ability to follow rules and cope non-verbally with others. The ability to play is considered to be a sign of mental health (Winnicott, 1971) and a prerequisite for creativity. Games with an element of competition without personal prestige in winning can increase motivation and improve the mood of the group. In interaction exercises, the patients try to adapt themselves to the group without giving up their personal integrity.

Reactions in the treatment process

Many physiotherapists working in psychiatry have reported a similar pattern of response from patients in Body Awareness Therapy. It has been described in three sentences, in many cases with identical words. The first comment is: 'I have noticed . . .'

(e.g. '. . . that I keep my head inclined'). This may represent an increased body consciousness. The second comment is: 'I have changed . . .' (e.g. '. . . the posture of my head, so I can see people I meet'), which may represent improved management of the body. The third comment is: 'I felt so . . . .' (e.g. 'free', 'happy'), which represents a deepened body experience. These comments might indicate that the influence of Body Awareness Therapy has reached the patient's consciousness, that the treatment was a self-experience, not just a body experience. This raises the question of possible effects of the treatment and how they might be evaluated.

Other methods in psychiatric physiotherapy

In clinical practice, a wide selection of treatment methods is necessary. Some of them are already well established in psychiatric hospital care in Scandinavia. Only a brief description will be given here.

Training of physical fitness

Since the 1950s a tradition of physical training has developed in psychiatric care in Sweden. The general goal of physical training was to keep the body healthy and maintain motor ability until mental health was restored. Specific goals were to keep or regain an adequate function of the respiratory and circulatory systems, general endurance and muscular strength. Physical training has by tradition been directed towards physical aspects where as psychological reactions received very little interest. This is now changing with an integration of physical training with the total treatment programme.

Relaxation techniques

Hypertensed muscles are seen as one element in a complex picture which includes imbalance in muscular tone, posture and breathing. Relaxation techniques are therefore incorporated into physiotherapy. The aim is to increase awareness of one's muscular tone, and harmony and balance in muscular tension in general. Hypertonic muscles are often relaxed as a result of non-specific physiotherapy. Even activities like dancing or exercises lead to relaxation in hypertonic muscles.

Relaxation techniques such as Jacobson's Progressive Relaxation (1948), Schultz' Autogenic Training (1960) and relaxing elements from Concentrated Movement Therapy (Goldberg, 1974) are used in a more or less modified form as part of the treatment. Since relaxation of hypertonic muscles may set free strong emotional reactions, especially agony, relaxation therapy has to be given with great care.

Massage

Massage and other contacts with the body influence those who receive and those who give the massage in various ways. Even if some research has been done in the field, clinical experience is the main source of inspiration for the following thoughts on the techniques and effects of massage:

1. Massage is communication. The therapist takes care and sends messages, especially the question: 'How are you?' The patient receives the care and answers by reactions in breathing, muscular tension and reactions in the skin.
2. Massage confirms the person (the receiver) through his body. The fact that the therapist agrees to touch the patient includes an aspect of accepting him as a person.
3. Massage can stimulate inner processes. A rhythmic pressure directed towards deep levels of the body can stimulate processes such as postural activity, breathing and digestion.
4. Massage can reduce both muscular and inner tension. It is not necessary to give relaxing massage as local therapy. Tension headache is often reduced by foot massage or treatment on the calf muscles.
5. Massage can lead to passivity and regression of the patient. Relaxation and rest can increase the patient's access to his resources, but it might also make the patient passive and dependent. In these cases massage should temporarily be avoided, or maybe combined with independent exercise.
6. Massage can stimulate the body's production of endorphins. This increases the feeling of well-being and is pain-relieving.
7. Massage can lead to increased tension in hypotonic muscles. Techniques for this purpose are being developed in, for example, Norway (Bunkan Heir, 1979).

8. There are techniques which work with special tissues or are directed towards autonomic reflexes. Correctly used, however, they influence the whole body and the patient's psychic life. Some examples are 'Bindegewebemassage', Rolfing and Acupressure. Few of these methods are yet in frequent use among Swedish physiotherapists, but they seem to be gaining increasing interest.

The above merits of massage as a therapeutic means in psychiatric care have become increasingly clear during the past few years. These possible effects can occur even for physiotherapists who are not very conscious of these aspects. They work mainly on intuition and often get good results. The therapeutic quality, however, is more controlled and on a higher level if the physiotherapist consciously uses different possibilities and techniques in her massage.

Psychomotor treatment

There has been a tradition of psychomotor investigation and treatment in Norway since Wilhelm Reich. Formal education created by Aadel Bülow-Hansen and developed further by Berit Heir-Bunkan and others has been given throughout Scandinavia.

Methods from other therapeutic fields

Many body-directed treatment methods have been developed outside psychiatric institutions. Some of them have been shown to be useful in psychiatric physiotherapy and interest in their educational and clinical use has been increasing.

The Alexander technique

The Alexander technique (1932, 1941) was developed by an Australian actor, F. M. Alexander (1869–1955). Its goal is to improve posture and harmony in the movements of everyday life. Alexander developed a technique for movement training aimed at influencing the person's pattern of movement as a whole, with the posture of the head and neck as starting points. The Alexander Technique is taught by specially trained teachers.

The Feldenkrais method

The Feldenkrais method (1949, 1972), developed by M. Feldenkrais (1907–1984), is in fact two training systems, one for individual treatment (functional integration) and one for group training, called Awareness Through Movement. The goal of Awareness Through Movement is to re-activate coordinations which are lost in present-day (mis-) use of the body or as a result of injury. The method often starts with a small movement which during several repetitions develops into a coordinated pattern that engages the whole body. This kind of training requires total concentration. Feldenkrais called his technique a body–mind method.

Laban art of movement

R. Laban (1971) developed his art of movement from the art of dance. He constructed a system to describe elements in movements such as time, space and flow. These elements of description have been shown to be useful even as therapy and are now used by many physiotherapists.

Concentrated movement therapy

Some body-centred therapies are mainly directed towards psychotherapeutic effects, such as bioenergetics (Lowen, 1971) and some elements of dynamic pedagogics (Lipschütz, 1971). Concentrated Movement Therapy (CMT) (Goldberg, 1974; Roxendal, 1981) provided most inspiration for psychiatric physiotherapy in Sweden through the repeated courses by Miriam Goldberg from Tel Aviv. It is a non-verbal psychotherapeutic method which was developed in central Europe in the 1920s. CMT starts from a total perception of the body and from the patient's healthy resources. Its aim is to increase self-knowledge and awareness, concerning both individual resources (self-esteem) and personal conflicts. Discharge of built-up energy and outflow of evoked effects are important elements in the method. Verbalization is also an important part of CMT, which is mainly used in Western Germany and Sweden.

Planning of treatment sessions

Every treatment session in psychiatric physiotherapy contains three elements: an introduction, a working phase and a conclusion. For individual settings one hour per session is the most common amount of time used. For group therapy one and a half hours is more frequent.

It is possible to treat from both a short-term and a long-term perspective. For in-patients, treatments twice a week or even every day might be useful for a period of intensive therapy. Out-patients are usually treated once a week. This makes it possible for patients to exercise independently between therapy sessions.

The different time perspectives also influence the length of a therapeutic intervention. Ten sessions are common for short-term therapy. Since the change in patients is often profound, long-term therapeutic processes also occur. Several years of continuous or recurrent contact are needed in many cases.

There are, however, no special rules for frequency of treatment and amount of time needed. The therapy follows the progress of the patient. Often it has to be adapted to practical conditions such as access to a gym and additional treatments.

CLINICAL APPLICATION

The physiotherapeutic domain in psychiatric care is concerned with different groups of patients. Since there are only a few physiotherapists compared to the number of patients, priority has to be given to some of the most important tasks. In many cases the physiotherapist works indirectly with the patient, i.e. supervising other members of staff. Application of treatment methods and cooperation within the team is described below.

Psychogeriatric patients

Like other areas of psychiatric care in hospitals geriatric wards are decreasing in number and most patients are being moved into nursing homes for somatic long-term care. In the remaining psychogeriatric wards there are three main tasks left for the physiotherapist: traditional physiotherapy in the case of injuries or motor dysfunction, primary motor training to maintain motor ability and in-service education for the nursing staff.

Traditional physiotherapy is adapted to the special needs of the patients. It is of particular importance to try to reach those patients who have lost their speech. They still have a need for contact and many of them express themselves clearly in a non-verbal way. Motor function to be trained can very well be instructed verbally with tactile impulses.

Primary motor training

It is clear that all psychogeriatric patients have a need for body movements. There is a system of movement exercises, worked out for elderly in-patients, called Primary Motor Training (PMT). It is based on the motor function needed for everyday life in a hospital ward. The basic level of PMT includes turning (while lying), sitting up in bed, standing up (from the bed or from a chair), turning while standing, etc. It also includes exercises for body perception, such as putting hands on head, on shoulders, on knees; and spatial exercises, such as walking in different directions, movements to the left and to the right.

There is also an advanced level of PMT including lying on the floor, standing up from lying on the floor, climbing up on benches, walking up stairs, dancing, etc.

Both levels include presentation exercises, singing simple songs and playing simple games.

Primary Motor Training is used with elderly chronic patients in order to maintain as much self-confidence and motor function as possible (Roxendal, 1987).

In-service education

The physiotherapist's contribution to the care on long-term and psychogeriatric wards is primarily in-service education for the nursing staff. Common subjects to be taught are ergonomics, e.g. for prevention of low-back pain, handling techniques in daily nursing and primary motor functions for elderly patients. The motor function of patients often decreases without an underlying physical disorder. Some patients, for instance, lose their ability to stand and walk independently without known cause. We call this loss of abilities 'psychomotor artefact'. Specific handling techniques have been developed with the aim of helping patients maintain their basic motor abilities. These handling techniques are used by nursing staff but they are taught and supervised by physiotherapists (Roxendal, 1980).

Long-term hospital care

Patients in long-term hospital care have often lost their motivation to move and the ability to take initiatives. But their need for physical activity is great in order to avoid the results of a physically and mentally passive life. The physiotherapist helps staff members look for activities that can interest patients with the aim of regaining their motivation for some kind of exercise and raising the level of activity in the ward. Different activities can be chosen for different patients and situations, such as gymnastics, dance, games, outdoor sports, etc. These activities can often be led by non-qualified staff under the physiotherapist's supervision. This training includes social elements which can have unspecific positive effects on patients' social behaviour. Traditional physiotherapy for physical problems is needed in long-term care as it is for other psychiatric patients.

Short-term psychiatric care and open care

Modern psychiatric care is increasingly changing into teamwork with several professionals in mental health teams. A physio-therapist is not always included in the team. If she is it is often not under the same conditions as the other mental health workers. The physiotherapist's contribution is specialized in such a way that she cannot be replaced by any other mental health worker. Nor can she, without an additional qualification, replace, for instance, a psychologist or a psychiatrist. The physiotherapist often belongs to at least two different teams, which means that she is not a full member of any team. She is, more or less, an expert, available for both the teams. The physiotherapist has to adapt to the philosophy of the teams, that is she might have to adapt to different therapeutic philosophies.

If the physiotherapist is responsible for many wards (8−12 wards with 16−24 patients in each is not an unusual number (1986)), she will have to work as a consultant. Thus she will be in regular but not daily contact with staff and patients. A large part of her work will inevitably be evaluation of the patient's symptoms, dysfunctions and resources. She may suggest training that other mental health workers can carry out with patients, such as movement exercises or other activities supervised by nursing staff or a gymnastic instructor.

Patients will receive physiotherapy individually or in groups. Often a period of physiotherapy starts with individual treatment and ends with group therapy. Physiotherapy is integrated into the patient's general treatment programme. The overall goal of therapy is decided within the team and physiotherapy is part of the total treatment.

The long-term goal for a schizophrenic patient may be an independent social life, if possible with his own flat and work. The physiotherapeutic part in this may be a re-established body ego (getting rid of schizophrenic body image aberrations), improved hygienic habits, normalized muscular tension, a higher level of daily activity and increased non-verbal communication.

Treatment methods for these goals would probably be Basic Body Awareness Therapy, first in individual settings and later on in a group, Expressive Body Awareness Therapy, and moderate training for physical fitness. The patient should finally be supervised in some activity he chooses outside hospital in the community, e.g. swimming or dancing.

FINAL COMMENT

Psychiatric physiotherapy is very much a process of communication where the interaction between patient and physiotherapist contains the main therapeutic power. To be able to take part in an effective meeting, the physiotherapist must work to develop her own identity. She should concentrate on the question 'Who am I?' The patients need to meet 'somebody'. Many physiotherapists in Sweden go through therapies of different kinds for their personal development. Some of them have completed a training in psychotherapy.

Many have chosen to learn and practice Tai chi chuan which originally came from China. Tai chi chuan is a classical form of movement training which also contains training in mental concentration. The methods and philosophy of Tai chi chuan are the source of knowledge for Body Awareness Therapy. Physiotherapists who train in Tai chi chuan for their own needs have described a growing capacity to inspire their patients to achieve increased autonomy and activity.

REFERENCES

Alexander F M 1932 The use of the self. Dutton, New York
Alexander F M 1941 The universal constant in living. Dutton, New York
Aasberg M, Perris C, Schalling D, Sedwall G 1978 The CPRS, development and application of a psychiatric rating scale. Acta Psychiatrica Scandinavia; Suppl. No 216
Bunkan Heir B 1979 Undersökelse og behandling ved muskelspenninger. Universitetsforlaget, Oslo
Carlsöö S 1968 Människans rörelser. PA-rådet, Stockholm
Dropsy J 1973 Vivre dans son corps. EPI, Paris
Dropsy J 1984 Le corps bien accordé. EPI, Paris
Feldenkrais M 1949 Body and mature behaviour. International University Press, New York
Feldenkrais M 1972 Awareness through movement. Harper & Row, New York
Fenichel O 1945 The psychoanalytic theory of neurosis. W W Norton & Co, New York
Fisher S, Cleveland S E 1958 Body image and personality. D van Noostrand Co Inc, New Jersey
Goldberg M 1974 Über meine Therapieformel in der Konzentrativen Bewegungstherapie. Praxis der Psychotherapie (No 6)
Horwitz T, Kimmelman S, Lui H H 1979 Tai Chi Chuan, the technique of power. Rider & Co, London
Jacobson E 1948 Progressive relaxation. University of Chicago Press, Chicago
Johnsen L 1975 Integrert respirationsterapi. Universitetsforlaget, Oslo
Laban R 1971 The mastery of movement. McDonald & Evans, London
Lipschütz D 1971 Dynamisk pedagogik. Wahlström & Widstrand, Stockholm
Lowen A 1971 The language of the body. Collier Books, New York
May P R A, Wexler M, Salkin J, Schoop T 1963 Non-verbal techniques in the re-establishment of body image and self-identity, a preliminary report. Psychiatric Research Report (no 16)
Østbye-Sundsvold M 1975 Muscular tension and psychopathology Psychotherapy & Psychosomatics no 26
Piret M, Beziers P 1979 La co-ordination motrice. Masson & Cie, Paris
Reich W 1945 Character analysis. Simon & Schuster, New York
Roxendal G 1980 Hander i Vårdarbete. Studentlitteratur, Lund
Roxendal G 1981 Levande Manniska. LIC-Forlag, Stockholm
Roxendal G 1985 Body awareness therapy and the body awareness scale, treatment and evaluation in psychiatric physiotherapy. Department of Rehabilitation Medicine, Göteborg
Roxendal G 1987 Ett Helhetsperspektiv, Sjukgymnastik infor Framtiden. Studentlitteratur, Lund
Schultz J H 1960 Das Autogene Trainung. Thieme, Stuttgart
Wen-Shan Huang 1974 Fundamentals of Tai Chi Chuan. South Sky Book Company, Hong Kong
Winnicott D 1971 Playing and reality. Tavistock Publ, London

5. Psychological factors in recovery from physical disability

C. Partridge

Patients with physical disabilities form a major part of the work of many therapists who well know the dilemma of trying to predict how each patient will progress, and to plan treatment programmes accordingly. Early studies describing patients with severe burns (Hamburg et al, 1953) and poliomyelitis (Visotsky et al, 1961) demonstrated the great individual variation in responses to physical disability with initial clinical severity on its own often a poor predictor of outcome. Experience and intuition, the present basis on which decisions are made, are crucial but it is not always enough to identify factors which may be influential in promoting recovery or find ways of helping those who seem to make little progress.

This chapter examines four factors which may contribute to a better understanding of the variable nature of the process of recovery from physical disability; the term disability is used here as in the International Classification of Impairments, Disabilities and Handicaps (WHO, 1980). This classification was developed to deal with the consequences of disease rather than the disease itself, and within it disability is defined as 'the restriction or limitation in the performance of the individual'; this differentiates it from Impairment, damage or loss at the level of organs and systems, and Handicap, the social impact of the disability or impairment on the individual's life-style. Because this paper focusses on physical disability there will be little discussion of diagnoses; while recognizing the importance of having knowledge and understanding of the pathology underlying the patient's condition, the emphasis here is on disability. In clinical practice patients with similar diagnoses may have widely different physical disabilities,

---

NB. The terms physiotherapy and physical therapy are used interchangeably throughout this chapter.

whereas patients with similar physical disabilities may have a variety of different diagnoses.

Though psychology per se has been given little weight in physiotherapy in the past — much less so than in occupational therapy — physical therapists have for many years used the language of psychology. The terms motivation, attitudes, responses, learning and attention are very frequently used by therapists in discussing patients and their problems. Yet there have been relatively few attempts to investigate the extensive literature in psychology dealing with concepts which could help to improve the general understanding of work with patients. Some aspects which have direct relevance for physical therapy will be explored.

Motivation

Motivation is a term frequently used by health professionals. Therapists, nurses and doctors talk of trying to improve their patients' motivation, and describing a patient as poorly motivated is often considered an adequate explanation for lack of progress. It is often mentioned in literature on the treatment of patients with physical disability in a wide range of diseases and conditions, by O'Gorman (1975), Stewart (1975), Hawker (1975), Brewin & Shapiro (1979) and Shepherd (1979). Because motivation is an internal experience and cannot be studied directly, its existence and nature are inferred from observation and experience, and underlying motives for behaviour are often difficult to define and classify. This perhaps is why research has been sparse in the field of human motivation, though numerous investigations of animal motivation have been reported.

To understand the concept of motivation it may be helpful to go back to its physiological origins. A person or animal is motivated to find food or water if deprived of it; physiologically, motivation is related to need. This situation is fairly clear cut and is associated with the concept of drive. The person or animal deprived of food may for the first hours have only a moderate hunger drive; this will get stronger as time passes. The motivation and underlying drive for food will reach a plateau; eventually apathy will take over as the individual becomes weakened because of lack of food and will eventually, without food, die. Here motivation is related to biological need and survival. Homeostasis, a state of balance and equilibrium, is necessary for effective functioning of any organism and there will be motivation, based on imbalance in physiological states, to restore balance if it is lost.

For example, salt is a necessary component of the diet of grazing animals, and if salt blocks are made available cattle are motivated to seek the salt and will avidly lick the blocks, this particularly so when mineral salts are not available in their diet. So physiologically there is an in-built motivation for survival and maintenance of balance for effective functioning of body systems.

Where basic physiological mechanisms are not involved other higher level cognitive thought processes and social motivation come into play. Murray (1938) introduced the concept of psychogenic needs relating to human motivation, differentiating them from biological and homeostatic needs. The comprehensive list of psychogenic needs was originally derived through observations both in daily life and clinic settings. They were presented under six headings and included such aspects as ambition, achievement, defence of status, avoidance of humiliation, affiliation and acquisition of knowledge. Maslow (1954) stressed that these needs are not necessarily at a conscious level, and may give rise to behaviour not obviously linked to a particular need. Any behaviour may be influenced by a number of different motives. Some aspects of motivation in human beings have been investigated, and those practically applicable in physiotherapy will be discussed.

Achievement motivation

This may be associated with a variety of goals and is defined by McClelland (1965) as activity directed towards the attainment of some standard of excellence. Individuals are thought to differ in the extent to which they see achievement as important, and tests have been developed called Thematic Apperception Tests (TAT, Stein, 1955) where the individual is asked to interpret a picture depicting a scene. It is intended to reveal basic themes that occur in the imagination of individuals; apperception means readiness to perceive in certain ways based on prior individual experience. From the results of these interpretations it is claimed that an individual can be rated on the strength of their achievement motivation. Vernon (1972) suggested that independence and achievement are closely related; achievement per se is not so important as achieving through one's own independent actions. It is important to remember that achievement motivation may not be aroused in every situation, only those which the individual perceives as important or where personal excellence is challenged. Regaining independence is a central feature in recovery from physical disability; and though little work has been undertaken with achievement motivation in the recovery of these patients, it may well be important to organize physiotherapy treatment sessions for some people in terms of a personally challenging situation rather than stressing the skills that physiotherapy treatment and management have to offer. The use of this kind of approach is supported by experimental evidence: Atkinson & Litwin (1960) reported finding greater persistence in their subjects high on achievement motivation when assigned achievement-related tasks rather than tasks where achievement was not stressed.

Affiliation

Affiliation has been described by Atkinson (1964) as concerned with the establishment and maintenance of positive affectionate relations with other people and a desire to be liked and accepted. Some conformity is necessary for social order but excessive conformity may arise from a strong need for approval. Recognizing this need for approval in some patients, which is sometimes overt, but may also be covert, should also help in understanding their behaviour and perhaps help in structuring treatment sessions in such a way as to maximize the effect for those who have a high need to be liked and accepted. Though it would not be possible to test each patient, being aware of the different types of motivation should enable therapists to respond more sensitively to their patients and realize that the therapy situation may need to be restructured if it does not seem to be arousing a suitable level of motivation in the patient. Different approaches may be needed with different patients. Though most therapists may do this intuitively, understanding more about possible sources of motivation should enable more effective interaction between therapists and their patients and clients by widening their repertoire of strategies for structuring and re-structuring the treatment situation.

Levels of aspiration

People frequently appear to set themselves some criterion of excellence — a standard they hope to attain — and the act of setting a level of attainment can of itself be motivating. A belief that the outcome in any situation is not contingent on personal efforts will have a profound effect on the level of aspiration:

believing the situation is controllable will raise the level of aspiration, and perceptions of uncontrollability and helplessness will lower it (Abramson et al, 1978). In a familiar situation levels of aspiration will be decided on the basis of past performance and the extent to which success or failure has been experienced; therefore it is important to ensure patients do perceive some success in early sessions. It is important that they actually perceive some success rather than receiving praise for trying hard. This was found by Partridge (1983) to be a source of considerable irritation for patients who reported 'I can see I'm not getting anywhere and they keep saying "you're doing well".' In a new or unfamiliar situation the individual's perceptions of the situation and the expectations of others may be more influential. Work in this area has very clear implications for goal setting in physiotherapy practice, structuring each patient's therapy in an individual way to achieve optimum results, setting goals that are appropriate and achievable with effort. Setting too low a goal, one that is too easily achievable, may reduce motivation in the future.

Knowledge of results

It has generally been accepted that knowledge of results of performance has two functions, firstly information about 'how I've done' and secondly motivational goal setting. Locke & Bryan (1967) found that those with specific goals based on past performance or assessments, performed better in experimental situations than those encouraged to 'do your best'. With differing instructions and feedback of information there were continual fluctuations in performance. To provide effective motivation, feedback of information about performance must relate to the individual's own goals or sub-goals, rather than those of the health care professional; and in the light of the constantly changing situation in recovery from physical disability, goals must constantly be re-set to appropriate levels depending on the rate of progress and the assessed potential of the individual.

Emotion

Emotion has an important part to play in motivation and Arnold's (1960) theory of emotion is defined motivationally; in terms of this theory, emotion is an externally aroused motive. The strength of the motive — the emotion — and task difficulty appear to interact. To a certain level emotion is facilitating but beyond that disruptive. The level at which it becomes disruptive is linked to task difficulty, more difficult tasks becoming disorganized at higher levels. Therefore, emotion may have both an organizing and disorganizing effect on behaviour; it can disrupt or produce new goal-directed forms of behaviour (Lazarus, 1963). An example is responding to frustration, which can include regression to childish behaviour, apathetic withdrawal or effective problem-solving behaviour. All these responses will have been observed in clinical practice in patients with physical disability.

Perhaps the information from experimental studies can help therapists to understand each individual's responses more sensitively and be able to restructure the situation in the light of greater understanding of the possible factors affecting each patient's motivation to overcome his disability. One of a therapist's tasks may well be trying to help the patient to keep his emotional responses below the level where they become disruptive. Folkman & Lazarus (1980) suggest an individual's main problem after the onset of illness may be to cope with the emotional reactions to it. Coping with the actual problems imposed by the physical disability comes after adaptive levels of emotional response have been achieved.

Many different factors may influence motivation during recovery and it is important to try to identify which factors arouse each individual's motivation so that strategies can be used which will enhance it. It is essential that goals of treatment are patient-oriented. Patients with stroke tend to have goals related to individual performance of functions in daily life, whereas therapists concentrate more specifically on movement or muscle problems related to aims of treatment (Partridge, 1985). Unless therapists' goals are openly linked to patients' stated real-life goals, there is little chance of them being motivating. Finally, it must be said that poor motivation of itself should never be accepted as an adequate explanation for accepting poor progress; rather poor progress should be considered — if there are no other apparent physical or social reasons — as a cue that different strategies may have to be used to enhance the individual's motivation to recover, with perhaps a complete restructuring of the treatment approach.

Coping and appraisal

Therapists frequently voice opinions about the way that individual patients are coping with their physical disability and may well quote one patient as an example to another: 'See how well Mr B. is coping and he has the same problems that you have'. Another often overheard in conversations between health care workers is 'if only Mrs R. could have a sense of reality and see how things really are everything would be so much easier'. Both these examples suggest that coping and reality are seen as important aspects of recovery from physical disability, but their actual meaning is often unclear and they are viewed by health care workers from a professional-observer position with a strictly unified interpretation that some things are good, others bad.

Coping as a response to the threat of illness has been examined by a number of authors, including Rose (1975) and Wright (1960), and it is usually defined as a positive and adaptive response. However, Ray et al (1982) challenge the assumption that coping is by definition reality based and adaptive and suggest the term can refer to any action taken with the aim of minimizing the adverse impact of a situation problematic for the individual. The onset of physical disability may pose different threats to different individuals, the relevance depending on each individual's appraisal of his situation. On the basis of work by Hamburg et al (1953), Visotsky et al (1961) and Moos & Tsu (1977), Cohen & Lazarus (1980) include the following as threats perceived by patients: threats to life itself, threats to bodily integrity and comfort, self-concept, future plans, one's own emotional equilibrium and adjustment to new physical and social environments.

Individual appraisal of the onset of the illness is seen as a central feature and a critical determinant of coping by Lazarus & Launier (1978) and Folkman & Lazarus (1980). The two components of appraisal are defined by Lazarus (1966) as primary and secondary: primary referring to evaluation of what is at stake for the individual, secondary taking into account individual coping resources and available options. The two processes are not necessarily seen as sequential but as part of a continuing process each affecting the other; the situation is constantly reappraised in the light of new events or threats. Lazarus (1966) differentiated between threat and challenge on the grounds that threat emphasizes potential harm, challenge positive mastery or gain. These appraisal processes are not necessarily conscious or deliberate; they may also be unconscious or on the fringe of consciousness. Ray et al (1982) suggest that not only does appraisal provide feedback on the success of coping but can of itself be a form of coping.

The stress imposed by illness or any other event cannot be seen exclusively in terms of the objective definition of the situation, because the capacity of any situation to produce stress reactions also depends on the characteristics of the individual (Bettelheim, 1943). This again has often been observed in clinical practice where a condition which seems little more than a nuisance to one patient, causes great distress to another. Folkman & Lazarus (1980) in their study of coping in a middle-aged population found that how an event was appraised and its context were the most potent factors accounting for the coping variability observed.

Many authors have stressed the individual nature of response to illness and the different strategies used by those with similar conditions, including Lipowski (1970), Moos (1977) and Lazarus & Launier (1978). In these reports not only is individual variation stressed but the fact that strategies are not inherently adaptive or unadaptive. What is appropriate and adaptive at one stage of an illness for an individual may not be so at another, equally so for individuals. Depending on their appraisal of the situation, different coping strategies may be appropriate at the same stage of recovery.

Lipowski (1970) suggested that illness may be seen as an enemy or a challenge. Common strategies reported as found in medical settings and listed by various authors include confrontation, tension reduction, disowning responsibility and self-pity (Weisman & Worden, 1976). Others include information seeking, requesting reassurance, setting concrete and limited goals and finding a pattern of meaning in events (Moos & Tsu, 1977).

In a study of patients with physical disability Partridge (1985) reported little correlation between objective measurements of severity and individually rated severity. Analysis of interview material showed that the coping themes identified by Ray et al (1982) in cancer patients of rejection, control, resignation, minimization and dependency, were also found in these patients. Two other points from this study which provide insight into the situation concern patient reports, and examples of different strategies used by individual patients with a Colles' fracture. A man of 58 who had suffered a severe stroke exasperated staff because of his inability to see and accept the 'reality' of his situation. 2 or 3 weeks after the onset of the stroke, he continually said with a smile, 'Don't worry, I'll be back at work (as a garage mechanic) in a couple of weeks'. This man went on to make a reasonable recovery and went home to be independent, though not back at work 6 months later. About 8 weeks after his stroke he spoke reflectively about the early days in hospital. He said: 'The staff gave me such pitying glances when I said I'd be back at work in 2 weeks — they got really annoyed with me — of course I knew I wasn't going back to work but you need time to get used to the idea of changing from a working man to a cripple overnight — it helped me to talk about going back to work at that stage.' It was clearly adaptive for this man to be 'unrealistic' at this stage, but staff saw it as maladaptive. This seems to be similar to the 'middle knowledge' of Weisman (1972), knowing but saying things which appear contradictory for emotional stability and reassurance.

Another finding reported from this study (Partridge, 1985) was of female patients who had a wrist fracture and were attending for physiotherapy after the plaster splint had been removed, and who still had considerable physical disability in their hand. They were asked how they managed with dressing and they reported getting on their brassières was one of the most difficult of dressing tasks. Three different methods of coping with the problem were revealed in their reports. The three responses related to Ray et al's (1982) themes and were as follows:

1. Asking someone else to do it   *Dependence*
2. Not wearing a bra   *Minimization*
3. Putting the fastenings to the front   *Problem solving*
   to do them up and then pulling
   round to the back

Each solution seemed to work well for the individual concerned, so was apparently adaptive for them, though (3) would generally be seen by health professionals as 'best' and the most adaptive method of coping, and the one patients would be encouraged to do. But there is nothing intrinsically 'bad' about the other two methods.

There seems to be a need for recognition among health professionals that coping strategies of themselves are not inherently adaptive or maladaptive and therapists must be prepared to facilitate coping responses that are present, though perhaps when necessary indicating other possible ways of coping. Each individual will initially decide for himself even though this may not be a conscious process. Collaboration mentioned in other parts of this chapter is as essential here as elsewhere: if therapists are to help patients in the most appropriate way they must be sensitive to individual responses and not try to impose a pattern of response on the patient. Solutions ought to emerge as a result of discussion and co-operation; help given in this way is most likely to be acceptable and effective in facilitating the recovery process and the patients' adaptation to the physical disability imposed by their condition.

Compliance

Advice and instructions form a major part of physiotherapy treatment and management, particularly for patients with physical disability, but little is known about the extent to which patients follow this advice. Studies of doctor–patient interaction report non-compliance as common, and there is no reason to think the situation is any different in physiotherapy. Mayo (1978) draws attention to a number of implications of this lack of knowledge. Firstly, if the extent to which instructions are followed is not known, it is difficult to judge whether advice and instructions given are sound or not, i.e. that following them would result in speedier and more effective recovery; lack of progress may mean that patients are not following the advice, or that they are, but it is poor advice. There is also a potential waste of time if patients are not understanding or remembering the instructions they have been given because resolution of their problems may then be unnecessarily delayed. Another problem in compliance in physiotherapy is that patients are often required to learn new skills of performance, and unless the acquisition of the necessary skills is checked there may be no chance of following the advice to practise because the necessary skills have not been learnt. There is an extensive literature on compliance with instructions given by doctors to patients; this is mainly about compliance with taking medication, but it does have implications for physiotherapy practice, and has provided useful guidelines on general principles when giving health care are information.

   Though the word 'compliance' is the most frequently used in this context, it has an overly authoritarian sound, so the terms adherence, cooperation and collaboration are also used interchangeably by many authors. In physiotherapy where patients and therapists are working together to try and solve or ameliorate the patients' problems, patient 'adherence' to an agreed treatment regimen is probably a more accurate term.

Numerous studies of doctor-patient communication as reviewed by Ley (1982) show that a number of factors can increase patients' understanding and remembering of the instructions they have been given. These include using short words, avoiding the use of jargon, only giving a small amount of information at any one time, putting what is most important at the beginning, repeating the instructions a number of times, and asking the patient to repeat them, and, if appropriate, giving written information.

At a practical level there are three problems in adhering to physiotherapy programmes. Firstly, patients must understand and remember the instructions they have been given; they must have learnt the skill of performing the required movements or activities and then form the habit of carrying them out in their daily lives.

It is also important to check whether patients can recall what they have been asked to do, without prompting. In early exploratory work Partridge (1985), in observation of physiotherapists working with patients, found that when checking if patients had been following instructions given to them the therapists themselves frequently gave prompts, or asked if it had been 'done like this', giving a physical demonstration, which the patient agreed with. Without these prompts and cues in a study sample of 40 patients with physical disability only 8 patients (20%) could accurately recall or demonstrate any instructions they had been given after some weeks of treatment.

Non-verbal communication can also have an important influence, and studies by Korsch et al (1968) in paediatric settings showed that if doctors appeared friendly and interested this enhanced the likelihood of mothers remembering instructions they had been given and following the advice in the care of their children. Blackwell (1973) concluded in an overview of the topic that the most important contributions to compliance were the understanding a patient has of his illness, the need for treatment and the likely consequences of both. This emphasis on patients' individual perceptions of the situation as necessary preconditions for compliance are further developed in the Health Belief Model (Becker & Maiman, 1975). This model asserts that current dynamics within the individual are the most important influence on health-related behaviour. The theory argues that whether or not an individual will undertake a recommended health action depends on four aspects: (1) the perceived level of personal susceptibility to the particular illness or condition; (2) the perceived degree of severity of consequences (organic and/or social) which might result from contracting the condition; (3) the perceived potential benefits or efficacy of the health action in preventing or reducing susceptibility and/or severity; and (4) the perceived physical, psychological, financial and other barriers or costs related to initiating or continuing the advocated behaviour. The perceived efficacy of the treatment, and the possible benefits, must outweigh perceived costs for compliance to be likely. The revised version of the model outlined by Becker & Maiman (1975) includes in addition the necessity of cues to action. These cues can include mass media campaigns, advice from others, one's own symptoms or reminder postcards. Without such triggers, beliefs of themselves may not be so influential in changing or eliciting certain health-related behaviours. A considerable volume of research supports the main suppositions: a belief in susceptibility to a specific disease correlating with participation in screening programmes (Fink et al, 1972) and immunisation (Ogionwo, 1973); the individual's own perceptions of the severity of the condition, and the costs and benefits of undertaking health-related behaviours in terms of finance (Antonovsky & Kats, 1970), or negative side-effects (Kirscht & Rosenstock, 1977); the subjective evaluation of costs in relation to resources. This research has implications for physiotherapy, but more research needs to be done to test the models in physiotherapy itself, as the original work and much of the research that has been undertaken has been in the area of preventive health behaviours and health education rather than behaviour when illness is present.

Another area of research that has implications for physiotherapy practice and adherence to agreed regimens are the techniques used in behaviour modification programmes. Success in a number of different situations has been reported: for example, prompts and reminders in paediatric practice (Shepherd & Moseley, 1976), contingency contracting (Mahoney & Thoreson, 1974), self-monitoring (Johnson & White, 1971) and reinforcement (Mann, 1972).

Measurement of compliance is difficult and presents many problems, both conceptual and methodological. The situation is complex in physiotherapy as the advice refers to actions in daily life rather than the taking of medication. Here counts of pills left in the bottle and urine tests for traces of the drug, or a marker given with it, seem more simple and bias-free, but even these methods which appear to be direct and objective are subject to error. The pills not in the bottle may not have been taken by the patient, and urine only sampled once or twice cannot claim to be representative of overall behaviour. Direct observation has been used, but introduces all the problems associated with changes in behaviour under observation. Patient reports are often used but must be interpreted with care: patients may often over-estimate the degree to which they are following the advocated regimen to please the clinician. Checking patient compliance is important, not only to find out the extent to which patients are following advice, but also as Svarstad (1974) has shown, because this demonstrates to the patient the importance the clinician places on compliance and this enhances its likelihood. This is clearly a very important though often neglected area of practice and one which certainly needs more attention in physiotherapy. Time spent talking to patients, getting to know them and explaining about their treatment and management may well be one of the most important aspects of effective physiotherapy though there is a tendency sometimes for this aspect to be seen as wasting treatment time. If giving more individual attention with carefully structured patient sessions does result in greater adherence to the home programmes, this will surely benefit the patient. Research needs to be undertaken to investigate the extent of patient adherence to physiotherapy regimens and the effects that this has on outcome.

PERCEIVED CONTROL

Extensive research has shown that people differ in the extent to which they believe that they themselves have control over their life in general, or in a particular situation. Early work by Rotter (1966) and others has described a continuum between internality, believing that positive or negative events in life are a consequence of one's own actions and thereby under personal control, or the other extreme, externality, referring to the perception of positive or negative events as being unrelated to one's own behaviour. More recently this theory has been studied in relation to health behaviours.

Early experimental studies examining learning under skill and chance conditions demonstrated that where tasks were perceived as requiring skill by the subjects of the study, i.e. that they themselves could effect the outcome, they behaved in more adaptive ways and achieved more than when the tasks were described as dependent on chance or luck. Lefcourt (1972) reported that perception of more internal control was related to the incidence of effective goal-striving behaviour, whereas more apathetic withdrawal occurred when subjects perceived other factors as controlling the situation. It must be emphasized that it was individual perception of control that was influential rather than actual control — this was demonstrated experimentally by giving the same task to two groups of subjects but varying the experimental conditions so that one group saw it as a controllable task, others as uncontrollable (Glass & Singer, 1972).

There have been a large number of scales developed to measure perceived locus of control. Throop & McDonald (1971) list 13 scales of measurement, but probably the most widely used is still that of Rotter (1966) which is seen as a measure of generalized expectancy which tests the dispositional or personality aspect. It consists of 29 free choice items such as the following. (3a) One of the major reasons why we have wars is that people don't take enough interest in politics. (3b) There will always be wars no matter how hard people try to prevent them. (2a) Many of the unhappy things in people's lives are partly due to bad luck. (2b) People's misfortunes result from the mistakes they make.

In 1978 Wallston & Wallston produced a Health Locus of Control scale (HLC) as an area-specific measure of expectancies regarding locus of control for prediction of health-related behaviour. The scale consists of 11 items, 6 internal and 5 external. The subjects are asked to express agreement or disagreement with the items on a 6 point rating scale. This again is a broad general measure and was constructed for use in predicting the undertaking of preventive health behaviours. Items such as (1) If I take care of myself I can avoid illness — an internal item — and (3) Good health is largely a matter of good fortune — an external item — are included.

The original theorists Rotter (1975) and Phares (1976) suggest that if it is an individual's perception of control in a specific situation that is required it may be necessary to construct a scale with items referring to that specific situation. A recovery locus of control scale (RLOC) has been developed to examine perceived control over recovery from physical disability by Partridge (1985). This is a 9-item scale with 5 internal items such as: 'Getting better now is a matter of my own determination rather than anything else', and 4 external items such as: 'It's often best to just wait and see what happens'. Items are scored on a 5 point Likert-type scale from strongly agree to strongly disagree. The scale is scored in the direction of internality; validity and reliability data are available.

Wallston & Wallston (1978) conclude in a review of the health literature that greater internality, i.e. a greater belief in personal control, is associated with the likelihood of engaging in behaviours that facilitate well-being. James et al (1965) found non-smokers more likely to be more internal; and subjects who had stopped smoking were found to score higher on internality than those who continued to smoke (Steffy et al, 1970). These relationships are also reported in weight-loss programmes, but there seems to be some interaction between the orientation of the programme and the extent of weight loss. Balch & Ross (1975) found that those deemed more external using the Wallston (HLC) scale lost more weight on an externally oriented programme, whereas those more internal only achieved weight loss with an internally oriented programme. This suggests a possible reason why some patients seem to make a lot of progress while others receiving similar treatment seem to make little progress. It also provides food for thought in planning treatment programmes.

Though there have been few rigorous studies investigating physical disability and perceived control, there are suggestions that a relationship may be found. Finlayson & Rourke (1978) reported finding a relationship between higher internality and motivation in treatment; this in turn related to outcome. However, the weakness of the study was that both motivation and outcome lacked clear definition and were based on therapists' subjective judgements. Lipp et al (1968) investigated the perceptions of normal subjects viewing photographs of disabled people. Those who showed more external orientation, as measured by Rotter's 1966 scale, were less denying of disability than more internally-orientated subjects. McDonald & Hall (1971) also found different relationships between internality and externality and physical disability.

In a small study of 40 patients with physical disability, Partridge (1985) reported finding that the extent of perceptions of internal control in her subjects was significantly related to outcome in terms of physical performance. Those who expressed a greater belief in personal control over recovery (RLOC scale) achieved more in terms of performance than those who perceived themselves as having little or no control over their recovery from physical disability.

If these results are replicated in further studies, it may be shown to be an important variable to be considered in recovery from physical disability. The way the health care situation is usually structured is with the professional as the 'expert', the person with knowledge who will 'get the patient better'. Indeed, this is often the specific purpose the patient is given. It seems that the most useful approach in physical disability may well be to have the emphasis on the professional's role as helping patients to achieve their objective. It remains to be tested whether beliefs about perceived control can be manipulated in this way.

Patients with physical disability are mainly the responsibility of therapists. Mulley (1985) says of stroke patients 'once the early days of the illness have passed there is a tendency for medical interest to wane . . . especially if the patient is "difficult" ' and this is true for most patients with longer-term disabilities. Since it is clear that there is great individual variation in response to physical disability, it would be to the patients' advantage for those who try to help them to have a greater understanding of the associated psychological phenomena as well as the physical problems. Though lip service is given to treating the 'whole patient' in practice this is rarely the case.

This chapter has raised a number of issues which may be important in the treatment and management of patients with physical disability, and in particular draws attention to the extensive literature in psychology which is applicable to physiotherapy practice.

REFERENCES

Abramson L Y, Seligman M E P, Teasdale J D 1978 Learned helplessness in humans. Journal of Psychology 87: 49–74

Antonovsky A, Kats R 1970 The model dental patient. Social Science and Medicine 4: 367–380

Arnold M B 1960 Emotion and personality. Columbia University Press, New York

Atkinson J W 1964 An introduction to motivation. Van Nostrand, Princeton, NJ

Atkinson J W, Litwin G H 1960 Achievement motive and test anxiety conceived as motive to approach success and motive to avoid failure. Journal of Abnormal and Social Psychology 60: 52–63

Balch P, Ross A W 1975 Predicting success in weight reduction as a function of locus of control. Journal of Consulting and Clinical Psychology 43: 119–121

Becker M H, Maiman L A 1975 Sociobehavioural determinants of compliance with health and medical care recommendations. Medical Care 13: 10–24

Bettelheim B 1943 Individual and mass behaviour in extreme situations. Journal of Abnormal Social Psychology 38: 417–452

Blackwell A 1973 Drug therapy patient compliance. New England Journal of Medicine 2: 249–253

Brewin C, Shapiro S 1979 Beliefs about self and their importance for motivation in rehabilitation. In: Osborne D J, Bruneberg M M, Eiser J R (eds) Research in psychology and medicine, vol 2. Academic Press, London

Cohen F, Lazarus R S 1980 Coping with stresses of illness. In: Stone G C, Cohen F, Adler N (eds) Health psychology: A handbook. Jossey Bass, London

Fink R, Shapiro S, Roester R 1972 Impact of efforts to increase participation in repetitive screenings for early breast cancer detection. American Journal of Public Health 62: 328–336

Finlayson M A J, Rourke B P 1978 Locus of control as a predictor variable in rehabilitation medicine. Journal of Clinical Psychology 34: 367–368

Folkman S, Lazarus R S 1980 An analysis of coping in a middle aged community sample. Journal of Health and Social Behaviour 21: 219–239

Glass D C, Singer J E 1972 Urban stress. Experiments on noise and social stress. Academic Press, New York

Hamburg D A, Hamburg B, De Goza S 1953 Adaptive problems and mechanisms in severely burned patients. Psychiatry 16: 1–20

Hawker M 1975 Motivation in old age: the physiotherapist's view. Physiotherapy 61: 182–184

James W H, Woodruff A B, Werner W 1965 Effects of internal and external control upon changes in smoking behaviour. Journal of Consulting Psychology 29: 127–129

Johnson S M, White G 1971 Self-observation as an agent of behavioural change. Behaviour Therapy 2: 488–497

Kirscht J P, Rosenstock I M 1977 Patient adherence to anti-hypertensive medical regimens. Journal of Community Health 3: 115–124

Korsch B M, Guzzi E K, Francis V 1968 Gaps in doctor-patient communication. 1. Doctor-patient interaction and patient satisfaction. Paediatrics 42: 855–71

Lazarus R S 1963 Personality and adjustment. Prentice Hall, Englewood Cliffs, NJ

Lazarus R S 1966 Psychological stress and the coping process. McGraw Hill, New York

Lazarus R S, Launier R 1978 Stress-related transactions between person and environment. In: Pervin L A, Lewis H (eds) Perspectives in interactional Psychology. Plenum Press, New York

Lefcourt H M 1972 Recent developments in the study of locus of control. In: Maher B A (ed) Progress in experimental personality research, 6. Academic Press, New York

Ley P 1982 Giving information to patients. In: Eiser J M (ed) Social psychology and behavioural science. Wiley, London

Lipowski Z J 1970 Physical illness, the individual and the coping process. Psychiatry in Medicine 1: 91–102

Lipp L, Kolstoe P, James W, Randall H 1968 Denial of disability and internal control of reinforcement. Journal of Consulting and Clinical Psychology 32: 72–75

Locke E A, Bryan J F 1967 Goal setting as a means of increasing motivation. Journal of Applied Psychology 51: 120–130

McDonald A P, Hall J 1971 Internal-external locus of control and perception of disability. Journal of Consulting and Clinical Psychology 36: 338–343

McLelland D C 1965 The achievement motive. Appleton Century Crofts, New York

Mahoney M J, Thoreson C E 1974 Self-control power to the person. Brooks Care, California

Mann R A 1972 The behavioural therapeutic use of contingency contracting to control adult behaviour problems — weight control. Journal of Applied Behavioural Analysis 5: 99–100

Maslow A H 1954 Motivation and personality. Harper & Row, New York

Matthews D, Hingson R 1975 Improving patient compliance. Medical Clinics of North America 61: 879–889

Mayo N E 1978 Patient compliance: practical implications for physical therapists. Physical Therapy 59: 1083–1089

Moos R H (ed) 1977 Coping with physical illness. Plenum Medical Book Company, London

Moos R H (ed), Tsu V 1977 The crisis of physical illness: an overview. Coping with physical illness. Plenum Press, New York

Mulley G P 1985 Practical management of stroke. Croom Helm, London

Murray H A 1938 Exploration in personality. University Press, Oxford

Ogionwo W 1973 Socio-psychological factors in health behaviour. International Journal of Health Education 16: 1–16

O'Gorman 1975 Anti-motivation. Physiotherapy 61: 176–179

Partridge C J 1983 A study of recovery in patients with conditions involving specific physical disability. Report No. 47, Health Services Research Unit, University of Kent at Canterbury

Partridge C J 1985 Cognitions and emotions as predictors of recovery in conditions involving physical disability. Unpublished doctoral thesis, London University

Phares E J 1976 Locus of control in personality. General Learning Press, Morristown, New Jersey

Ray C, Lindop J, Gibbons S 1982 The concept of coping. Psychological Medicine 12: 385–395

Rose M H 1975 Coping behaviour of physically handicapped children. Nursing Clinics of North America 102: 329–39

Rotter J B 1966 Generalised expectancies for internal versus external control. Psychological Monographs 801 609 (whole): 1–28

Rotter J B 1975 Some problems and misconceptions related to the construct of internal versus external control of re-inforcement. Journal of Consulting & Clinical Psychology 43: 56–67

Shepherd R 1979 Some factors influencing the outcome of stroke rehabilitation. Australian Journal of Physiotherapy 24: 173–177

Shepherd D S, Moseley T A 1976 Mailed versus telephoned appointment reminders to reduce broken appointments in a hospital outpatient department. Medical Care 4: 268–273

Steffy R A, Meichenbaum D, Best J A 1970 Aversive and cognitive factors in modification of smoking behaviour. Behaviour Research and Therapy 8: 115–125

Stein M I 1955 The thematic apperception test, rev edn. Addison Wesley, Reading, Mass

Stewart M C 1975 Motivation in old age. Physiotherapy 61: 180–182

Svarstad B 1974 The doctor-patient encounter: an observational study of communication and outcome. Unpublished doctoral dissertation, University of Wisconsin

Throop N F, McDonald A P 1971 Internal–external locus of control: a bibliography. Psychological Reports 28: 175–190

Vernon M D 1972 Human motivation. University Press, Cambridge

Visotsky H N, Hamburg D A, Goss M E, Lebovits B V 1961 Coping behaviour under extreme stress, observations of patients with severe poliomyelitis. Archives of General Psychiatry 5: 423–448

Wallston B S, Wallston K A 1978 Locus of control and health. A review of the literature. Health Education Monographs 6: 106–117

Weisman A D 1972 On dying and denying. A psychiatric study of terminality. Behavioural Publications, New York

Weisman A D, Worden J W 1976 The existential plight in cancer. Significance in the first 100 days. International Journal of Psychiatry in Medicine 7: 1–15

Wright B A 1960 Physical disability — a psychological approach. Harper & Row, New York

World Health Organisation 1980 International Classification of Impairments Disabilities and Handicaps, WHO, Geneva

6. Rehabilitation of torture victims: physiotherapy as a part of the treatment

I. Bloch & G Møller

HISTORICAL BACKGROUND

In 1975 the World Medical Association defined *torture* as the deliberate, systematic or wanton infliction of physical or mental suffering by one or more persons acting alone or on the order of an authority, to force another person to yield information, to make a confession, or for any other reason.

For millennia, torture was accepted as the right of rulers to protect the establishment of the society, its citizens and its divine institutions against crime, or just deviations from the generally accepted mode of life and thinking. What today is included in the generally accepted concepts of torture was a legally-based practice in many countries until the 17th century, and it was not completely forbidden until the 19th century. Today torture is not prescribed in any law, and yet torture is practised to an increasing extent in several countries throughout the world.

The methods of torture are refined. New technology is constantly being developed, and, increasingly, torture combines physical and psychological mutilation.

Torture has been called a social cancer of an epidemic nature. Thinking of the many national and international conventions and laws which condemn torture, it is a tragic fact that the use of torture is increasing. More than 60 national governments use torture against their own citizens, and at the same time they deny the existence of it.

As a result, international organizations and individuals struggle to counteract this sad development. Prevention of torture has become a social issue of paramount importance.

Amnesty International held a conference on The Abolition of Torture in December 1973 to discuss how to verify that torture had taken place and how to abolish the practice.

A main topic of discussion was the sequelae of torture, and this led to the formation of a group of Danish doctors in 1974, on the initiative of Inge Kemp Genefke, whose aim was to conduct basic research into the late manifestations of torture. It is a fact that doctors are involved in planning torture, both in deciding how much the individual can tolerate, and in refining torture methods, mainly to prevent the appearance of late objective manifestations. Only a similar professional group with the opposite conviction would be qualified to verify allegations of torture where particularly sophisticated techniques were used. In brief, the Amnesty International Danish Medical Group's main objective was to accumulate information about torture, so that conclusive evidence could be presented wherever torture had occurred, thus supporting the United Nations Universal Declaration of Human Rights.

No medical group like this had ever been formed before, so no empirical material was available. Its organization and method of working had to be developed without an existing model. Since then more than 1000 torture victims have been examined by physicians and more than 4000 physicians in 28 countries are now attached to Amnesty International medical groups.

The mandate of the doctors sent by the Amnesty International's Executive Committee was to examine victims and, where possible, confirm or reject torture allegations, as well as to collect material for further research.

A comprehensive study of torture methods was the first part of the programme, followed by application of clinical and ancillary studies designed to relate particular torture techniques to their specific late sequelae.

The investigations have revealed that torture victims are suffering from several psychological and physical torture sequelae. The most severe sequelae are of a psychological nature comprising depression, anxiety, reduced memory and concentration capacity, tiredness, headaches, irritability, sleep disturbances and sexual problems.

In 1978 Amnesty International held a seminar: 'Violation of Human Rights — torture and the medical profession'. On this occasion an international group of 14 physicians and lawyers was established to take action against the above problems. It was concluded that rehabilitation of torture victims was an obvious responsibility for the medical profession and that this activity was not within the framework of Amnesty International.

ESTABLISHMENT OF RCT

At a meeting in London in 1980 it was decided to ask the Danish members of the group to establish the first rehabilitation centre for treatment of torture victims. By the beginning of 1980 the Danish Medical Group had already been granted permission to accommodate and treat 5–10 torture victims free of charge each year at Rigshospitalet, the University Hospital of Copenhagen.

An interdisciplinary group at Rigshospitalet consisting of doctors, nurses and physiotherapists started developing therapeutic models. In the autumn of 1982 the non-profit-making, independent, humanitarian institution, International Rehabilitation and Research Centre for Torture Victims (RCT), was established. Official inauguration took place on May 5, 1984 — symbolically, on the 39th anniversary of the Liberation of Denmark in 1945.

The Centre has at its disposal two houses close to the University Hospital. Any resemblance to an institution is avoided as far as possible, i.e. the interior is decorated and furnished more like a home, and the staff do not wear uniforms. In principle most of the treatment takes place at the Centre on an out-patient basis. Only comprehensive examinations or operations are done at the University Hospital where two beds at the Department of Neurology are at the disposal of RCT.

The permanent staff consists of: physicians, psychotherapists, physiotherapists, social workers, nurses, a librarian, secretaries and administrative staff (today 27 persons). In addition, there are part-time staff: interpreters, dentists and consultants within different medical fields. Half of the budget is covered by the Danish Government; the other half is funded by various private donations and contributions nationally and internationally.

The rehabilitation programme of RCT is offered to refugees, their spouses and children, provided the refugee has been subjected to torture and has obtained asylum in Denmark.

The objectives of RCT

— To run a centre for the rehabilitation of people who have been subjected to torture and their families.
— To instruct Danish and foreign health personnel in the examination and treatment of people who have been subjected to torture.

— To engage in research on torture and on the nature and extent of its consequences for the purposes of treatment and eventual abolition.

— To set up an international documentation centre for the purposes of disseminating facts about torture, studying the consequences of torture and rehabilitating people who have been subjected to torture.

The admission procedure

A torture victim who has been referred to the centre will first be asked to come to a detailed interview. If the person is a torture victim and eligible for treatment he/she will undergo the standard examination programme which consists of:

1. A detailed examination by a psychotherapist. This will often take place over 3 sessions, each of a duration of 2−3 hours. A few psychological tests are included.
2. A clinical examination, including a neurological examination.
3. An examination by a social worker.
4. An examination by a rheumatologist.
5. A dental examination.
6. An examination by a nurse, including an ECG, a urine test and various blood tests.
7. An examination of the spouse.
8. An examination of the children.

THE TORTURE AND ITS SEQUELAE

To understand the consequences of torture one must have precise information about the methods applied.

Previously the purpose of torture was to punish and obtain information that was useful to those in power. The development of new, gruesome and perverse torture techniques within the last 15 years demonstrates that today torture has an entirely different aim. Increasingly specific and refined psychological techniques are used, developed by doctors and psychologists.

Today the aim of torture is the destruction of the identity of the victims.

Torture falls into three major categories:

1. Physical torture

Fig. 6.1 Blows on the skull while hanging on the 'parrot perch'

2. Psychological torture
3. Pharmacological torture.

Physical torture can be:

— *Blows on the skull* with rifle butts, kicks etc. causing
headache. On palpation the galea is usually adherent
generally or locally, and even a light touch of the skull
induces pain (Fig. 6.1).
— *Blows and kicks* on the trunk and extremities. After torture
haematomas may occur. Sequelae may be scars, adherent
tissue and muscle pain. Fractures, when untreated, cause
osteoarthritis. Other sequelae may be backache due to
fracture of the spine.
— *Falanga* is blows to the soles of the feet. Late sequelae will be
pain and difficulties in walking. Palpation may reveal fixed
tarsal bones, a taut sole and myogenic changes in the lower
legs (Fig. 6.2).
— *Exposure to electricity*: to all parts of the body causing
muscular pain; applied to the teeth this will cause loosening
of the teeth which will fall out.
— *Burning* with lighted cigarettes: scars on the skin.
— *Submarino*, where the head is forced into water filled with
hair tufts, vomit etc. and held there almost to the point of
suffocation. As a sequela there will be infection in the
mouth and gingivitis.

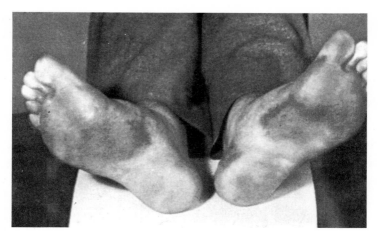

Fig. 6.2   Feet one week after falanga torture

Fig. 6.3   Suspension

— *Suspension* by the hands in mid-air often for days, either with the hands above the head or behind the back: complaints of articular as well as tendon and muscle pains (Fig. 6.3).
— *Prolonged standing*, often for days, which later results in problems with the lower legs: pain and oedema.
— *Teléfono* is beating on both ears at the same time. This may later cause impaired hearing or even deafness.

Psychological torture is associated with all types of torture.

Examples of psychological torture are humiliation, sham executions, witnessing torture sessions, sleep deprivation, continuous exposure to light, solitary confinement, total sensory deprivation, threats agaist the victim or his family.

The psychological sequelae after psychological torture are: anxiety, depression, fear, irritability, memory and concentration loss, sleeping difficulties, nightmares, headaches, emotional instability or outbursts, change or confusion in self-perception and body awareness, sexual disturbances.

Pharmacological torture is enforced application of psychotropic or other drugs.

GENERAL PRINCIPLES OF EXAMINATION AND TREATMENT

The most important goal is to restore the victim's personality in order to enable him to take responsibility for his own life again and to return to normal physical and social activities; i.e., to restore a sense of human dignity, so that he can learn to recognize and accept his own body and its functions, and to release emotional strain in a creative manner.

Before RCT was established 35 victims were treated in the hospital, and the knowledge obtained about physical and mental sequelae to torture was used to develop principles and guidelines for treatment.

It became obvious that it was disadvantageous to treat the victims as ordinary patients, and that it was extremely straining for the victims to be hospitalized. In the process of examinations and treatment, consideration had to be given to the type of torture the victim had been exposed to.

An unexpected difficulty was, for example, that doing an ECG could frighten the victim so much that he would suffer from tension and anxiety. The reason was that the procedure for doing an ECG was similar to the preparations for electrical torture. For victims who had been soaked in their own blood or seen their friends bleeding, drawing of a blood-sample could be traumatizing. The waiting time before entering an examination or treatment can be extremely disturbing, because part of the torture was just waiting either inside or outside the torture chamber for the torture to begin, exposed to the screams from other victims.

The psychological sequelae place the client in the role of a victim also in relation to the therapist which means the victim is not able to change his own position without help.

In physiotherapy it was necessary to be very gentle without using any instruments. Some of the victims reacted with anxiety or total refusal to participate in pool therapy. The reason was that the victim had been exposed to the torture called 'Submarino'. Traction of the spine can cause great anxiety because it reminds the victim of being strapped down under torture, and apparatus with electrodes reminds him of electrical torture. Taking off a shirt can be very stressful, because the victims may have been forced to take off their clothes in front of the torturers.

Other aspects of the surroundings can cause anxiety: flickering fluorescent tubes, certain colours, noise or people wearing white coats.

The treatment at RCT is interdisciplinary and the fundamental principles are:

1. The therapy shall be both physical and mental, and these two aspects of care must be offered simultaneously with psychotherapy and physiotherapy as the cornerstones.
2. Procedures which may evoke the re-living or the memory of torture experiences shall be avoided as far as possible.
3. The scope of the treatment must include children and spouses.
4. Social conditions have to be taken into consideration, and a personal social service shall be part of the treatment.

The following is a brief outline of the various treatments, the physiotherapy treatment being described in more detail. *The general somatic treatment* is individual of course. Many torture victims suffer from gastritis or ulcus duodeni. These clients receive traditional medical treatment and only rarely is surgery performed.

Nursing consists to a large extent of personal counselling, support and information. Above all, very thorough information is given about the various somatic examinations and treatments. An important part of the nurse's work is instructing the client about diet and nutrition.

All exiled torture victims have social problems. *Social counselling* is a multi-faceted job where torture victims are involved. One of the first priorities is that the social worker, in cooperation with the client, helps solve housing, financial, employment-related and educational problems.

Psychotherapy normally starts with $1\frac{1}{2}$ hour sessions twice a week. Interpreters are used for the majority of sessions. The point of departure for psychotherapy is torture which the victim has been exposed to. The psychotherapist tries to make him/her understand the aim of torture, i.e. destruction of the victim's personality (identity), and to recognize that all the responsibility and guilt must rightly be placed with the torturers.

In torture situations a victim is faced with a series of impossible choices which mean that other people will be confined and tortured no matter what the torture victim answers to the interrogator's questions: 'If you do not give the names of your friends (who would be arrested and tortured if he did) we will arrest your wife and children and torture them'. A realization of the 'impossible choice' helps free the victim of his/her sense of guilt.

The victim must express suppressed feelings of anger, grief, hatred and rage — feelings experienced during torture but which had to be hidden. The victim cannot forget but must learn to see the torture as a thing of the past. Talking about torture arouses strong resistance. It is painful but the situations must be recalled, reviewed and relived.

It may take a long time and call for patience and many explanations but, above all, it requires the establishment of a sustained relationship of confidence and trust. Once the resistance is broken down, the treatment is incredibly easy.

Different methods are used to achieve the goals. In therapy a person's dreams are often used as the basis. Most of the clients have nightmares about imprisonment and torture. Other methods are used, for instance presentation of water colour paintings depicting torture situations, drawing therapy and role play. The methods of treatment are continually being developed and improved because of the influence of the many different cultures and various consequences of torture.

Dental treatment. Many torture victims have had their teeth broken or pulled out; some have had their jawbones crushed. Lack of oral hygiene in the prison may have caused dental caries or parodontosis. Traditional dental treatment will be given based on a knowledge of the torture the client has been exposed to. The dentist will carefully instruct the client about what he is doing and take care that the client is under anaesthetic for all painful procedures.

Spouses are offered an interview and examination, and the necessary treatment is initiated. Most often this will consist of remedying physical problems and through counselling seeking to solve family-related problems.

Children are a vulnerable group and RCT has chosen to give high priority to the examination and treatment of children. Often these children suffer from psychosomatic disturbances. The centre's social worker, paediatrician and perhaps the psychotherapist contact the relevant social authorities, schools, youth centres, kindergartens, etc. In some cases actual psychiatric/psychological treatment is necessary, but often the child can be treated in cooperation with the parents, the social worker at RCT and the paediatrician.

PHYSIOTHERAPY

Physiotherapy is an important part of the entire treatment which is offered to torture victims at the RCT. Well-known physiotherapeutic methods and techniques are applied on the basis of an awareness of the correlation between man's physical and mental health.

Physiotherapy is used to overcome physical pains and symptoms which are a constant reminder of the prison and torture experiences. By respecting the reactions and bodily signals of the client, the client's confidence in him-/herself, in others and the experience of self-esteem and respect are rebuilt.

The emotions which are a consequence of the torture, e.g. anxiety, anger, grief and resignation, the physiotherapist can see in the client's pattern of muscle tension and body carriage. Many clients have a changed body awareness; the anger and hatred will often be focussed on the place where the sequelae of torture are found, or the client may reject the entire body or parts of it.

Examples

One female client had been severely sexually tortured. When she came out of prison and saw herself in a mirror she only saw her face — she did not want to/could not feel nor see the rest of her body.

Another client lay strapped to a concrete floor in the prison for weeks, and because his metal buckle dug into the skin on his back, he made his back insensible. At the examination there was a belt-shaped eczema and the musculature in the loin was atonic and dead in spite of the fact that the client otherwise had very tense muscles in the rest of his body.

Principles of physiotherapeutic examination and treatment

1. The most important thing in planning physiotherapeutic examination and treatment is a thorough knowledge of torture methods in general. Specifically we must know what kind of torture the individual client has been exposed to, so that we avoid situations and methods which may resemble the prison or torture situation, as this creates fear and distrust. For example, we must closely consider which initial positions we use during examination and treatment.

   — Inspection of the client's carriage in a standing position half-dressed is not possible from the start.
   — Supine position on a couch may cause anxiety and unrest.
   — Treatment with electric instruments brings back memories of electric torture. (However, we use ultrasound, but only after close consideration and acceptance by the client; this applies to TNS — transcutaneous nerve stimulation.)
   — Pool treatment may remind the client of submarine torture, and traction of the spine may bring back memories of having been strapped down under torture.
   — One must be aware that any kind of touching may cause anxiety.

2. It is necessary to inform the client thoroughly of the physiotherapeutic treatment, preferably through an interpreter. It is important to bear in mind that the clients may not be familiar with physiotherapy. Perhaps they have only encountered health staff in connection with torture or attempts to remove traces of its use. Interpreters are used, especially in the beginning, and later when deemed necessary. It is important that the client formulates his/her problems and experiences in his/her own language.

3. As far as possible the treatment should be within the pain limit, as the purpose is to give confidence and provide good physical experiences and to relieve pain.
4. During treatment the physiotherapist must be aware of body signals and reactions and ask questions about these, since autonomous reactions and muscular tension are the physical expressions of emotions. Furthermore, it may be necessary to assure the client of the physiotherapist's professional secrecy. During treatment it is also necessary to be aware of the influence of cultural and other factors on clients' attitude to treatment, i.e. clients' expectations of treatment, their attitude towards the therapists, their understanding or lack of knowledge of the body–mind relationship, their different attitude to male and female rôles and dressing/undressing in the treatment situation.
5. The treatment is based on interdisciplinary cooperation. It is of great importance that the treatment team (psychotherapist, physiotherapist, social worker, nurse) is kept constantly up-to-date on the client's situation, so that the treatment can be coordinated and adjusted continually. This is done at a weekly meeting at the RCT.

The treatment builds upon generally known physiotherapeutic methods and techniques, taking previous torture and prison experiences into consideration. The physiotherapist should be sympathetic and professional but not sentimental. In principle physiotherapy takes place twice a week for one hour. The entire treatment period lasts from 8 to 12 months.

Physiotherapy case 1

A 49-year-old Latin American male, unemployed, lived by himself in an apartment; his family remained in the home country.

He was tortured during several imprisonments in the course of about 15 years. He was held in isolation for two years and also subjected to mental torture by threats to and abuses of his family, and had been subjected to countless mock executions.

Methods of torture used included:

— Long stays in a cold, damp cell without furniture, mattress etc. This caused rheumatic muscle pains.
— Blows and kicks to the entire body, especially in the heart

region and to the soles of the feet. Once he was hit with an iron rod which broke his left clavicle and caused haematomas and pains all over his body.

— Teléfono, causing reduction in hearing of the left ear.
— Suspension on the 'parrot perch'. While on it he was beaten and kicked over the entire body, including the genitals. This caused pains in the joints, dysuria and haematomas.
— Electrical torture to the genitals, teeth and extremities.

While in prison the client was told he suffered from hypertension which was treated medically. He also had a tendency to faint, as well as suffering from anxiety, depression, nightmares and hallucinations.

An examination one year after prison showed the following physical complaints, which were assumed to be sequelae of the torture described:

— Constant pain on the left side of the thorax. The pain had been present since the first torture session about 16 years earlier. Palpation revealed myogenic changes in the left pectoral region and tenderness to the touch at the third to sixth rib on the left side. An X-ray showed sequelae to a fracture of the left clavicle.
— Myogenic changes in the neck region, interscapular region and lumbar region which were tender to even a gentle touch.
— Fatigue and pain in the feet after walking a short distance. Palpation showed the soles of both feet to be very taut and the tarsal bones to be fixed.
— Daily headaches which were intensified by touching the cranium. The galea was found to be sore and adherent to the entire scalp.
— Other complaints: tension, insomnia, depression, anxiety, reduced memory, reduced ability to concentrate, and nightmares.

The following physiotherapy treatment was given:

— The client began with exercises in the pool. He had not been subjected to submarine torture; the water was 35°C. The pool treatment was discontinued after 20 treatments. The client had fewer symptoms from myogenic changes in the dorsal region, and could now tolerate being touched and massaged.
— In the same period ultrasound was applied to the soles of

the feet as well as articulation, mobilization and exercises for the joints of the feet. After treatment the client was able to walk 4 km without pain.

— Headache treatment involved gentle loosening of the galea. After 23 treatments he no longer suffered from headaches.

— Relaxation exercises of the muscles in the neck, preceded by hot packs and instruction in relaxing the neck and shoulder muscles at home.

— Instruction in back exercises.

— The pains on the left side of the thorax were treated with ultrasound and massage. Even after 25 treatments, however, no further improvements were seen. The painful area had been considerably reduced, but the client still complained of a 'piercing' pain in a specific part of the pectoral region.

The client did not wish to receive a muscular injection by the rheumatologist. Through an interpreter, TNS (transcutaneous nerve stimulation) treatment was explained to the client. Even though he had been subjected to electrical torture, he agreed to try this treatment. By this time he had so much confidence in the therapist that he was certain that he could terminate the treatment immediately if he became too uncomfortable. After 12 treatments the constant pain had disappeared and only hard pressure could cause pain.

Simultaneously with physiotherapy the client was offered psychotherapy with a psychotherapist. The treatment lasted for 4 months. As he improved physically, the client also noticed a mental improvement. He felt less tense, slept better and had become more spontaneous in his thoughts and actions. In addition to doing exercises at home as prescribed, he took up jogging on his own initiative.

Physiotherapy case 2

Mohammed is a 33-year-old single male from the Kurdish area of Syria. He lived at home until he was imprisoned when he was 30 years old. He is a teacher and has worked as such for 10 years. He has been politically active for several years and is a prominent member of his union.

The torture and imprisonment took place during a period of 2 years. Before the sentence was passed — which was for 20 years — he was released for a short time. He immediately went underground and in 1985 came to Denmark as a political refugee.

Imprisonment

Mohammed was arrested at the school where he worked and his arms were tied together in front of his body. He was taken to a military camp nearby where he was immediately blindfolded and placed in a room with approximately 50 others. The prisoners had to sleep on a concrete floor without any blankets, even though it was ice cold at night. They also had to relieve themselves on the floor. Mohammed was blindfolded for 3 months. Interrogation and torture took place in long sessions lasting approximately 8−10 hours at intervals of 1 week so that he could recuperate.

Torture

On arrival in the torture chamber he was undressed. He was beaten and kicked everywhere. He was bent double and placed in a car tyre which was suspended from the ceiling, and he was then subjected to falanga (beatings on the soles of the feet). Such beatings are transmitted to the head and give the sensation that the head is about to burst. Furthermore, sitting crouched up in a tyre makes it difficult to breathe. He was also strapped to a metal bed and then placed upright and subjected to electric torture to the toe nails, penis, rectum, ears, hands and nipples. At the same time he was sprayed with cold water. Cigarettes were put out on his scalp. His head was put in a toilet. One of his arms was chained to a wall for 2−3 days, so that he was forced to stand up for this entire period. He was forced to drink the water on the floor where the prisoners had been lying all day and had relieved themselves. He was forced to eat soap and toothpaste and to be smeared in faeces. There was no possibility of having a bath or dental hygiene during the entire period of imprisonment.

He was threatened that his family would be fetched and that his parents and sister would be tortured. He was also threatened with execution. Furthermore, he was threatened with being permanently injured — that he would be impotent for the rest of his life and that he would soon die due to the injuries he had acquired from the torture.

All methods of torture were accompanied by the mocking laughter of the guards. The prisoners were laughed at and they were forced to laugh at each other.

The intention was to turn the person into someone completely without self-esteem, without identity, to change an active human being into a passive victim.

Symptoms

When he arrived in Denmark he was depressive and anxious. He lived in a hotel with a number of other refugees but he completely isolated himself even from his own countrymen. He had nightmares in which he relived the torture and imprisonment, and woke up with pounding heart and covered in sweat. He only slept for a few hours each night. He attended a language school to learn Danish but had difficulty in concentrating on the teaching and could not remember what he had learnt. He was convinced that there was something severely wrong with him physically. All these symptoms are typical and are seen in almost all clients. Furthermore, he complained of:

Headache:	Throbbing intermittent, localized to the forehead as frequent fits lasting 15–30 minutes. In between the fits constant pressing headache localized to the whole head, especially to the back of the head and forehead.
Cervical pains:	Localized to the back of the head and the shoulders.
Facial pains:	Constantly felt tense in the musculus masseter.
Back and loin:	Pains along the whole spine which increased downwards, were worsened when the client stood for a long time. Could not carry any loads There was radiation along the os sacrum, but not into the legs.
Lower extremities:	Constant feeling of tension in both calves. Pains in both ankle joints and feet when he walked.
Objectively:	
Spine:	The thoracic kyphosis was increased, especially upwards; lumbar lordosis was somewhat flattened. There was no inhibition of movement in the loin, but pains on movement. The sacroiliac joints were free. On palpation of the spine there was soreness and fixation of the apophyseal joints in the

entire extent of the thoracic spine with positive skin rolling test.

Upper extremities: Normal neurological conditions with tendinitis around both shoulder joints.

Lower extremities: Hips and knees free, both ankle joints slightly fixed and medium fixation of tarsus. Soles of the feet were sore.

Palpation: Muscle tension in the shoulder girdle, cervical and masseter muscles, soreness corresponding to galea. Muscle tension in pectoral muscles, muscles of the back, quadratus lumborum, gluteus medius, gluteus maximus, piriformis. Furthermore very sore muscle tension in femoral and crural musculature.

The aim of the physiotherapeutic treatment was first of all to create confidence and then to try and remove (lessen) the pains,

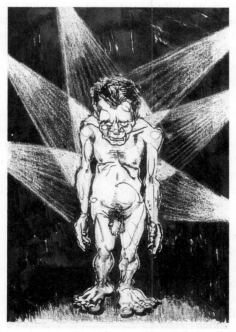

Fig. 6.4 Mohammed appears as the man in the picture, careful, poor body carriage, very little self-confidence

and to work with Mohammed's body to change his carriage and increase his self-esteem.

At the first treatment I asked him what bothered him most. Since the headache bothered him most I started by treating that. I placed Mohammed on a chair without a shirt and with a blanket around him. I placed myself on a stool next to him so that I had eye contact with him all the time. Sitting in this way I palpated the muscles in the neck and shoulders, partly to find muscular changes and partly to register Mohammed's reactions to being touched.

While I palpated the trapezius muscles Mohammed's eyes began to wander and he became very uneasy in the chair. Apparently he could not stand my touching his body.

So I placed him on a couch in the supine position with hot packs under his shoulders and gave him gentle massage of the galea, frontalis and temporal muscles. This relaxed him so much that he fell asleep. After approximately four treatment sessions I could begin to treat his shoulders and back with massage.

The treatment was supplemented by stretching exercises for the cervical muscles, respiratory exercises and mobilization of the thorax which was totally stiff. He had a very superficial, highly thoracic respiration. The headache was significantly lessened; he no longer had intermittent headaches with fits, but now and then still had pains in the back of the head and forehead.

The pains in the femora and crura were treated with massage and stretching exercises through the clothes, as Mohammed did not want to take his trousers off. Even though Mohammed had been tortured with electric torture I tried, naturally with his acceptance, ultrasound for the soles of the feet, as in our experience ultrasound is a good treatment for 'falanga feet'. However, ultrasound gave Mohammed such severe pains that I stopped and instead mobilized the tarsal bones and did various exercises for the feet.

The loin was treated with hot packs and massage. Furthermore I started working with various bioenergetic exercises and exercises for the pelvis in the lying and standing positions. Mohammed was totally blocked with regard to the innervation of the muscles around the pelvis, e.g. he could not actively contract the abdominal muscles at all. Little by little the muscles around the pelvis were loosened. When he stood he fell together a little so that he had a small 'potbelly'. One day he came and asked me if I had any exercises which could make the belly go away. It was tremendous progress for him to show an interest in his body and looks. I supported him in his interest and we concentrated on more exercises for the abdominal muscles and corrective exercises for his body carriage.

When we finished the treatment Mohammed no longer had pains in his head, neck and shoulders, back and legs. However, he can still get pains in his loin if he stands up for too long. His body carriage is improved, and he has been given a training programme for use at home which will improve his body carriage even more. He has started to cycle from his home to the school and back again every day, a distance of about 10 km, to improve his fitness.

He functions well, he maintains eye contact and he speaks Danish well. Socially he has started a Danish teacher training course and he teaches immigrant children their native language.

He received physiotherapy for 9 months and had approximately 50 treatment sessions of 1 hour each.

Parallel with physiotherapy treatment he went for sessions with a psychologist. The first sessions were characterized by a special kind of resistance where Mohammed had difficulty in suppressing his laughter when he talked about his torture and the prison. He said that it was necessary to laugh at everything in prison so as to be able to stand it. The guards laughed at the prisoners, they laughed at each other and at themselves. When it became evident to Mohammed that this was the guards' attempts at exercising psychological torture as part of the humiliation strategy, the smile stiffened and a long depressive phase began. Mohammed talked in detail of the torture and the prison in a low monotonous voice. It took place at the intellectual level; he was completely out of contact with his grief or anger.

One day Mohammed arrived severely shocked — he had just been told that one of his friends has been murdered in Denmark. As he was telling this he drew on a piece of paper. This prompted the psychologist to ask him to draw more images on paper for the next session — the contact improved a lot and gradually he opened up emotionally. In his own quiet way he showed the grief, anger and longing for warmth and humanity which he had not dared show before.

After approximately 8 months the therapy was completed. Mohammed sleeps well at night, is not depressive, is not anxious in the way he was before, and does not believe that he suffers from a somatic disease. He is able to concentrate and attend a further education course in Danish.

CONCLUSIONS

The results of the rehabilitation of torture victims have been very positive. The majority of the victims undergoing this treatment have seen their symptoms reduce or disappear completely.

Physiotherapy plays an important part in the rehabilitation of torture victims. The treatment methods applied are basic and well known to all physiotherapists. The methods have, however, to be carefully selected for each victim, not only to be able to treat specific problems, but also, most importantly, to avoid reminding victims of the torture they have experienced. Therefore, electric appliances (except sometimes ultrasound and TNS), traction when it involves fixation of the body, and often pool therapy, have to be avoided. Instead gentle massage, hot packs, relaxation exercises, stretching, exercises for improvement of body awareness (i.e. in the clients' acceptance of their body and to give them a feeling of pleasure from the body), ultrasound, breathing exercises, training of the muscles, stabilizing exercises, improvement of fitness and bioenergetics, are the most common treatment methods.

Physiotherapy, however, cannot stand alone as the only treatment. At the same time the client should undergo psychotherapy and receive assistance with social problems. Only then can the victim's life, family life and social activities become balanced.

Rehabilitation work has proved that torturers do not achieve their goals. Torture does serious damage but never destroys a person's identity completely. There will always be a core left which enables us to turn the victim into a whole person again.

Different activities

In 1983 two nurses from the neurological department at Rigshospitalet formed a club consisting of women from Latin America. The club meets regularly and has a social as well as an informative aim.

A group of male clients has created a club 'The Dawn Group'. The group is very active in work connected with cultural and social arrangements.

In the spring of 1985 RCT started, together with students from the Danish high school of gymnastics, activities including swimming, gymnastics, dance, theatre etc. twice a week for 15 children of RCT's clients. It has been a great success and will continue. Later, parents were able to participate in the swimming lessons.

There is a pottery at the RCT; the potter is a former client with RCT and he teaches the children and other clients the creative art of how to make pottery.

There are also classes in cookery. Apart from being a social get-together, the course has an educational purpose. The clients are taught how to do the shopping and how to cook, which is what many young men, for example from the Middle East, are unable to do.

Teaching

Teaching is another important objective of RCT. The informative and educative work is carried out for several reasons. The main target is medical and paramedical staff with the aim of establishing similar treatment around the world. In the long term, the disclosure of torture, its consequences, and the principles for rehabilitation of torture victims, should become part and parcel of the training of physicians and other health staff.

RCT has arranged five seminars in Copenhagen with 400 people participating from four continents. Three of the seminars were sponsored by the UN's Voluntary Fund for Torture Victims. Outside Denmark formalized tuition has been given in the Philippines, Kenya, Latin America, USA and Europe.

On the invitation of the World Psychiatric Association (WPA) RCT arranged a symposium at WPA's regional meeting in Athens 1985 and again in Copenhagen 1986.

One of the most significant results of RCT's international teaching is the establishment of treatment centres in other parts of the world. Centres have been opened in Sweden, France, the Philippines, Latin America and USA.

Because of national teaching a broad section of health staff know about the methods and consequences of torture as well as the rehabilitation of torture victims.

For medical students at the University of Copenhagen a chapter on 'Medical aspects of problems connected with human rights', including in particular torture and its consequences, has been incorporated into the medico-legal curriculum. This year physiotherapist students will start learning about this subject.

At an international meeting in the Netherlands in 1986, sponsored by the World Health Organization (WHO) and partly arranged by RCT, WHO supported the suggestion that a course on the rehabilitation of torture victims should be part of the curriculum for all health personnel. This point of view has been communicated to the Governments in Europe by WHO.

Research

Research is also an objective, and RCT is to engage in and promote research in to the nature of torture and the sequelae to torture with the aim of prevention and treatment.

In 1983 a scientific advisory committee was set up to advise the RCT board in respect of research-related issues. At present RCT is engaged in the following projects:

— A thesis on 'The Global Epidemiology of Torture' is at its conclusion.
— A controlled study 'Transcultural study of violent injuries' in cooperation with local doctors in the countries involved.
— A controlled study of mental problems in children of torture victims who are living in exile in Denmark and undergoing treatment at RCT.
— A pilot study of the sleep function of torture victims has been recently embarked upon.
— An interdisciplinary research project including more than 1000 different items entitled 'Torture victims, health, family relations and social conditions — a prospective study before and after treatment at RCT'. All information will be processed in a database.
— None of the projects is at present completed so no results are available. The results of the completed projects will be published in relevant medical journals just as many articles already have been.

Documentation centre

The documentation centre was the last objective of RCT. Recently RCT has undertaken this task, and the documentation centre has been able to serve the public since autumn 1987.

The objective of the docu-centre is to handle *bibliographic* documentation material on various aspects of torture, i.e. methods, sequelae and rehabilitation of victims. The docu-centre will not be dealing with medical records or urgent actions.

At present the docu-centre has collected and systematized approximately 2000 bibliographic units, books, journals and bulletins. The docu-centre has a small collection of videos and slides.

All the material is being catalogued into a database.

REFERENCES

Agger I et al 1985 Torture victims — on the psychotherapy of refugees who have been submitted to torture. The Nordic Journal of Psychology (Nordisk Psykologi) 37(3): 177–192. Danish title of original: Torturofre — om psykoterapi af flygtninge, der har været udsat for tortur

Barfoed G et al 1982 Physical therapy of torture victims. The Danish Physiotherapist Journal (Danske Fysioterapeuter) 19: 8. Danish title of original: Fysioterapeutisk behandling af torturofre på Rigshospitalet. Translated by RCT into English, Spanish

Bloch I 1988 Physiotherapy and the rehabilitation of torture victims. Clinical Management in Physical Therapy 8(3): May-June: 26–29

Bølling P 1978 Dental torture. The Danish Dental Journal (Tandlægeblade) 17: 571–574. Danish title of original: Tandtortur. Translated by RCT into English, Spanish

Cohn J et al 1985 A study of Chilian refugee children in Denmark. The Lancet. Aug 24: 437–438

Duarte A 1985 Annual Report 1984 Rehabilitation and Research Centre for Torture Victims.

Genefke I K, Aalund O 1983 Rehabilitation of torture victims. Research perspectives. The Danish Medical Journal (Månedsskrift for Praktisk Lægegerning) 51(1): 31–38. Danish title of original: Rehabilitering af torturofre. Forskningsmæssige perspektiver. Translated by RCT into English, Spanish

Genefke I K et al 1987 Rehabilitation of torture victims. Teaching. In: Health hazards of organized violence. Proceedings of a working group on health hazards of organized violence. Veldhoven Apr 22–25, 1986 Hague: Ministry of Welfare, Health and cultural affairs, pp 155–163

Jakobsen L 1985 Confidence and security are presuppositions for helping torture victims. The Danish Nurses' Journal (Sygeplejersken) 27: 4–7, 24. Danish title of original: Tillid og tryghed er forudsætningen for hjælp til torturofre. Translated by RCT into English

Kosteljanetz M, Aalund O 1983 Torture. A challenge to Medical Science. Interdisciplinary Science Reviews 8(4): 320–328. Translated by RCT into Spanish

Lunde I 1982 Mental sequelae to torture. The Danish Medical Journal (Månedsskrift for praktisk Lægegerning) 60(8): 476–489. Danish title of original: Psykiske følger hos torturofre. Translated by RCT into English, Spanish

Lunde I 1987 Rehabilitation of torture victims. Treatment and research. In: Health hazards of organized violence. Proceedings of a working group on health hazards of organized violence. Veldhoven Apr 22–25, 1986 Hague: Ministry of Welfare, Health and Cultural Affairs, 136–148

Rasmussen O V, Marcussen H 1982 The somatic sequelae to torture. The Danish Medical Journal (Månedsskrift for Praktisk Lægegerning) 60(3): 124–140.

Danish title of original: Torturens somatiske følger. Translated by RCT into English, Spanish

Somnier F, Genefke I K 1986 Psychotherapy for victims of torture. The British Journal of Psychiatry 149: 323–329

Svendsen G 1985 When dealing with torture victims, social work involves the entire family. The Danish Social Workers' Journal (Socialrådgiveren) 11: 8–11. Danish title of original: Socialt arbejde med torturofre involverer hele familien. Translated by RCT into English

Tornbjerg A, Jakobsen L 1985 Violation of human rights and the nursing profession. International Nursing Review 32(6): 178–180 & 1986: 3(1): 6–8

Ortman J et al 1987 Rehabilitation of torture victims: An interdisciplinary treatment model. The American Journal of Social Psychiatry VII 3, summer

All articles are available from The Documentation Center, RCT Juliane Maries Vej 34, 2100 Copenhagen Ø, Denmark

7. Integrating psychological factors into the physical rehabilitation of victims of torture and other abuses

T. Cimini

INTRODUCTION

In the preceding paper, Inge Bloch and Grete Møller have described the nature of the torture experience and its potential impact on both physical and psychological factors. Having noted that the methods are refined and are undergoing constant development, the comprehensive treatment plan and goals of the Research Centre for Torture Victims must focus on all of these aspects of the torture experience. With this as a foundation I would like to elaborate on some of the subtle consequences of torture and other abuses and their psychological effects.

Subsumed within a broad category of 'psychological sequelae' are (1) existential consequences of the torture/abuse experience; (2) psychic consequences relating to the structural basis of personality, and (3) neuropsychological/organic-cognitive aspects of direct trauma. Bloch and Møller cite the aim of torture to be 'the destruction of the identity of the victims' and the goal of rehabilitation to 'restore the victim's personality in order to enable him again to take responsibility for his own life and to regain normal physical and social activities.' To achieve this end the collective focus of the rehabilitation team must be trained on subtleties within each of these factors. I will discuss these factors separately as a means of providing basic definitions but the more important end goal will be to emphasize integration of all of these factors in treatment. Finally, before launching into the discussion I should like to frame the context from which I write. I am not an expert on torture. My observations are based not on research but on clinical experience in treating victims of torture and trauma. As a physical therapist (my original professional training) in the late 1960s and early 1970s this came in the form of treating American soldiers wounded in the Vietnam conflict. And now, as a neuropsychologist, part of my work involves evaluating patients who have suffered trauma, among them Indo-Chinese refugees, many of whom are the victims of torture as well. What I would offer is not 'expertise' (which implies that I am operating from a base of theory) but rather perspective on the integration of physical and psychological effects from the unique vantage point of one who has dealt with both.

EXISTENTIAL ASPECTS OF THE TORTURE/ABUSE EXPERIENCE

While it is necessary to understand the very specific features of torture, such as the means and methods used, it is also helpful to understand it as an experience of victimization. As such, the consequences extend far beyond the event itself and there are many common effects in the responses of victims regardless of the type of trauma. For example, victims of rape, child abuse, spouse abuse, or motor vehicle accidents, who are more commonly seen in general practice, might also experience these effects. In particular, a common consequence of the experience of victimization is the shattering of one's perception of the world as meaningful (Janoff-Bulman, 1985).

Phenomenologists have sought to determine the basis upon which we, as human beings, integrate ourselves into the larger context of the world around us. A basic model of the social world allows that experience is integrated and given meaning by the individual and, thus, the lived-world of that person takes form (Tymieniecka, 1962). Implicit in the attribution of meaning to experience is the process of relating other peoples' experience with our own for the purpose of interpreting the motives of their actions. It is here where the fault line lies for the victim of torture, for rarely is the torture experience one to which the victim can relate in any way. The fracture between their positive beliefs, hopes and wishes about the world and their interpretation of the intentions of the perpetrators of their pain can be so gaping as to seem irreparable. When we can no longer consciously organize our world in rational ways (this being the survival mechanism of the human animal) we are vulnerable to disintegration and estrangement not only from our social world but from our inner spiritual and psychic world as well. The existential reality we experience acts both as a guidepost for where we've been and a benchmark for where we are going.

Coping with the psychological effects of torture thus, necessarily, involves rebuilding a belief system which can act as a basis for reconstructing one's lived-world or assumptive world. Here it is not so important that those who are treating the patient understand the existential reality of the patient (for rarely is this even possible). Rather, the care giver must recognize the importance of allowing the patient to accept that a fracture has occurred so that the need for healing can be supported. Otherwise there exists the possibility that the patient will seek to control his emotional response rather than dealing with the 'environmental transaction' by which it was precipitated (Lazarus, 1977).

While it is not the primary focus of the physical therapy treatment, the more the therapist can acknowledge and accept the lived-world of the patient, the more room will there be for the individual to work toward his or her own reconciliation of the events.

PSYCHIC CONSEQUENCES OF TORTURE AND ABUSE RELATING TO THE STRUCTURE OF PERSONALITY

While it is still unclear as to precisely how the human personality is shaped, it is clear that as a structure it is vulnerable to disintegration. The destruction of the personality by the methods of torture is a response to stress which the individual must redefine in order to recover. There are many therapeutic methods for accomplishing this, but for the purposes of this discussion it is especially helpful to relate this new learning to the principles of Piaget (1971).

Children pass through certain invariant stages on the way to accomplishing new learning, and the first of these six stages is the sensori-motor stage of development. In this stage the child relates all new experiences to his physical senses. By experiencing new things on this very concrete level the child is able to relate them to something he or she already knows (his or her own body). It is then possible to lay down the beginnings of a cognitive map for forming a new percept which includes the new thing just learned. All learning is organized and reorganized for the individual as he or she moves through life: first in the concrete way described and later in more abstract ways. The sum total of these interconnected pieces of data results in the structures which underlie not only one's cognitive abilities but also one's personality. We become aware or conscious, if you will, of elements within our universe, and our consciousness becomes a factor which limits how we construct the universe.

As a result of the trauma of torture, the individual may repress the affective recollections of traumatic events and unwittingly make them no longer available to the conscious realm. While they may still influence the behavioural response of the individual (i.e. an unconsciously mediated fear response in the face of physical therapy treatment with modalities), they are unavailable to be put on the table for the working through which must be accomplished in psychotherapy. Thus, there may remain gaps in the structure of the individual's personality which fail to close as a result of the inaccessibility of the conscious connections which would allow for resolution.

Here, physical therapy is an especially powerful component of the patient's treatment, for the very concrete nature of the sensori-motor stimulation of the physical therapy treatment can help to lay down a matrix of primary trust in another person. This will enable the patient to move ever more steadily towards more abstract methods of reintegrating his or her personality in the light of a new consciousness.

The following case provides an illustration of how physical therapy can be of primary beneficial value in assisting the patient towards reintegration.

Case study

The patient is a 28-year-old married mother of three who initially presented at a local dental clinic with multiple complaints including chronic toothaches and pain in her jaw and neck. She was also morbidly obese and suffered from hypertension. Upon examination by the dentist, she was found to have severe deterioration of her gums and the bony tissue supporting her teeth. In fact, several teeth required extraction. The patient acknowledged a history of grinding her teeth and vaguely related some stressors in her daily life.

She was referred for psychological evaluation, and after an extended evaluation over several weeks she revealed that she was regularly beaten by her husband whom she said was 'under a lot of stress at work'. The couple had been married for 10 years and the beatings began after the birth of their first child 2 years after they were married.

It was clear that this patient was experiencing significant anxiety and depression, but she was unwilling to engage in psychotherapy to work through the many complex issues which faced her. Rather, since she was ridden with several significant physical signs and symptoms, she was able to engage in a multimodal physical therapy programme which included biofeedback and relaxation training.

By beginning to focus on self-mastery in the physical realm, this patient was guided towards success experiences that would enhance later exploration of her psychological needs.

NEUROPSYCHOLOGICAL/ORGANIC–COGNITIVE SEQUELAE

The cognitive sequelae of trauma are quite complex and often are very subtle. As Bloch and Møller have noted, psychological sequelae of torture include 'depression, anxiety, reduced memory and concentration capacity, tiredness, headache, irritability, sleep disturbances and sexual problems'. What can be complicating is that all of these symptoms are known consequences of traumatic head injury (Fishman, 1978). Beatings around the head can certainly accompany any experience of torture or abuse. Working in a centre such as was described by Bloch and Møller, where team evaluation and treatment are stressed, there is little risk of confusing the neuropsychological sequelae of head injury due to possible beatings with psychic trauma. But for the therapist working in isolation, the distinction between psychological consequences and neuropsychological consequences must be carefully considered.

A psychological consequence for the purposes of this discussion is one which is the result of an internal interpretation of an event or events, or an unconscious reaction to events such as to render the individual dysfunctional in some meaningful behavioural way. A neuropsychological or organic consequence is one which has a specific structural or neurophysiological aetiology based on what is known about normal brain-behaviour relationships. For example, following a traumatic head injury it is not uncommon to have a combination of clinical features including depression, anxiety, malaise, and a complex of mental status changes which significantly hamper one's ability to cooperate with rehabilitation efforts.

It is helpful to organize thinking about the function of the brain in driving human behaviour by considering dimensions of behaviours which interact to create our overall adaptive capacity. Intellective, affective and control functions (Lezak, 1983) are all coordinated within normal brain functions towards an end result which allows one to know what to do, for how long, by applying what techniques and in what circumstances. The fully integrated personality is one which allows the individual to make maximal use of her or his intellectual, emotional and physical abilities. The presence of organic brain dysfunction is a threat not only to the expression of these abilities but to the recovery of one's functional ability to use them.

For example, a well-known consequence of frontal lobe dysfunction is a resultant disinhibition and difficulty in filtering out unnecessary (and often intrusive) stimuli from one's frame of consciousness. This intrusive material might be from external sources or arising from within the individual's stream of thought. The difficulty which one has in the presence of frontal lobe dysfunction is that he or she *cannot* control these intrusions to turn them off. A tragic result for the torture or abuse victim who has suffered a brain injury as a result of beatings could be the inability to filter out the nightmarish recollections of the experience. Thus, they are locked into a mind set from which they cannot escape due to their lacking the cognitive apparatus necessary for working through. This can create a significant barrier to mobilizing the necessary resources to help a patient.

INTEGRATING THE PSYCHOLOGICAL AND NEUROPSYCHOLOGICAL CONSEQUENCES

The preceding discussion addresses some of the varying aspects of the psychological and neuropsychological effects of abuse and trauma. Beyond mere discussion of these factors, we must look for ways to integrate them into the physical therapy treatment of the victim. In doing so three major elements emerge as being crucial to the contribution of the physical therapist. First, the physical therapist is a critical link in re-building the personality of the patient given what is known about abstract cognitive concepts having their basis in growth in more concrete sensory awareness. Second, trust and rapport are more easily fostered first in the context of physical therapy. And third, that the pragmatics of human communication (that is touch, intonation, non-verbal communication) (Watzlawik, 1967) can serve as a critical link in bridging the understanding gap for someone who has suffered brain damage as a result of torture.

If we view re-learning through the same lens as we view the acquisition of knowledge, then the physical/sensate experience of the patient is going to be of great importance in helping him or her to re-establish a basis of trust in his or her world view. This writer is particularly impressed with how much the laying on of hands can facilitate a trusting relationship with a patient. As a psychotherapist I often lament how laborious a task it can be to cultivate trust in a relationship with a patient when it was so much more accessible in my experience as a physical therapist. The immediacy of touch which is experienced in the physical therapy relationship is in stark contrast to the more distant and, of necessity, abstract approach to building rapport in the psychotherapy relationship. Further, for the victim of torture or abuse, undergoing simultaneous physical therapy while psychotherapy is undertaken can provide the patient with valuable data to bring into his or her psychotherapy for discussion. The in-vivo exposure to re-integrating one's body awareness, combined with the desensitization which can be afforded by the therapy itself, is concrete material which the patient, with the help of the psychotherapist, can react to vis-a-vis his past or future expectations. In a case such as the one described previously, physical therapy might be the sole treatment initially until the patient builds a degree of trust and confidence. Finally, the pragmatic or non-verbal aspects of communication can help greatly with the patient who has suffered a brain impairment. We know that when given simultaneous verbal (syntactic) and non-verbal (pragmatic) messages, the human will attend first to the pragmatic communication. Thus, for the patient who cannot fully integrate the nature and tasks of his physical therapy by being instructed solely in words, pragmatic cues can provide him or her with a cognitive anchor in treatment.

SUMMARY

These additional thoughts with respect to integrating the psychological and neuropsychological effects of trauma with the physical therapy treatment of the patient are aimed at encouraging integration of these multifaceted effects. The victim suffers an existential schism in her or his concept of the lived-world of real experience. The event may be of sufficient impact or at a time in one's development when a significant effect on psychological and personality structure can result (indeed this is an aim of torture). Further the physical effects of the trauma itself can result in organic brain damage which further complicates the rehabilitation process by sabotaging one's adaptability and coping skills.

The physical therapist can influence the relearning process by providing concrete sensory experiences of trust and relatedness upon which the patient can build. In so doing, the physical therapist enjoys the enhanced opportunity to establish rapport afforded by the use of physical touch in treatment. And, where the patient is, by virtue of brain dysfunction, even more impaired in relating to his rehabilitation, the therapist can employ pragmatic communication to circumvent potential areas of misunderstanding: for example, in providing demonstration and waiting for the patient to respond versus explanation which might confuse the patient or cause her or him to misunderstand and reject treatment out of fear.

We are complex, all of us, regardless of our race or national origin. There are some things which regardless of our culture or religious beliefs are beyond what our human hearts and souls can reconcile. Torture is such a thing. Those who would rebuild the bodies and souls of the victims of torture are sharing in a work which might ultimately tell us much about the nature of man. The rubble left behind after the destruction of an edifice almost always reveals something of its nature in integrated form. Just as the foundations of buildings are created as the result of the interrelatedness of mortar and stone, the fully integrated and free human being is built of body and mind and spirit and can spare none of these ingredients in the process of reintegration after victimization.

REFERENCES

Fishman W A 1978 Organic psychiatry. Blackwell Scientific Publications, New York
Janoff-Bulman R 1985 The aftermath of victimization: Rebuilding shattered assumptions. In: Figley C R (ed) Trauma and its wake: study and treatment of post-traumatic stress disorder. Brunner/Mazel, New York
Lazarus R C 1977 Cognitive and coping processes in emotion. In: Monat A & Lazarus R (eds) Stress and coping. Columbia University Press, New York
Lezak M D 1983 Neuropsychological assessment, 2nd edn. Oxford University Press, New York
Piaget J 1971 Biology and knowledge. University of Chicago Press, Chicago
Tymieniecka A T 1962 Phenomenology and science in contemporary European thought. Polish Institute of Arts and Sciences, Poland
Watzlawik P, Beavin J, Jackson D 1967 Pragmatics of Human Communication. W W Norton, Inc, New York

8. Integrated Respiration Therapy: a function of wholeness

L. Johnsen

PROLOGUE

Kirsten Sandborg RPT
Stud. Cand. Polit. Social Anthropology
Physiotherapist, Lecturer at the College of Physiotherapy, Oslo

Lillemor Johnsen's therapy is interesting in an anthropological perspective because in order to understand it fully we must be aware of cultural differences.

Every culture organizes its own phenomena of reality. Culture is a result of the way reality is arranged. A new reality will be arranged according to the cultural pattern which is already established.

To organize is to classify phenomena. What is not arranged or classified looks like chaos; it is not understandable. The basis for this classification is shared knowledge within a culture which we communicate through codes or words.

Western culture is based on natural science laws. These have continually captured and organized reality and classified it. In doing this, focus has been placed on the parts, and this has become more important than the connected whole.

There are many who realise this fact, and within different disciplines there is work going on, trying to knit the parts together to a more cohesive whole. In this holistic wave physiotherapists are trying to unite psyche and soma.

But when it is said that 'the body's healthy and diseased functions are influenced by and influence psychic functions' (see p. 1), then it looks as though this fusion has not been very successful. The division is still there.

Lillemor Johnsen's way of understanding is rare, because it is not built on this dualistic concept of man divided into body and soul. These are the two parts which psychosomatic physiotherapy is trying to unite. She does not accept this. Since physiotherapeutic methods are based on this dualism, she does not want her therapy to be classified as such. Integrated Respiration Therapy is at the limit of what can be classified by means of our cultural codes. When phenomena go beyond already developed classes and concepts, we do not understand them.

When something cannot be classified so that we can understand it, we look for elements we can recognize in the unknown, because they

153

resemble others that we already know. That is the way we organize new reality. We grasp known elements in the unknown, or in chaos. Thus we make a class and a concept for them by looking for what is alike and not alike.

If we try to grasp L.J.'s knowledge and approach, by explaining, describing it mechanically and physically as a method, it will be classified and therefore understood in the same way as methods we already know. Instead we must try to grasp something we recognize, which is like something else, but without making it into something it is not.

As we cannot look at and learn L.J.'s therapy in the way we would with traditional physiotherapeutic methods, we have to stretch ourselves a little in order to be able to conceive of something for which concepts do not yet exist.

What is similar to physiotherapeutic methods in Johnsen's approach is that the starting point or medium is the body. It resembles physiotherapy. The next similarity is that L.J. too uses her hands, especially the fingertips, that she is 'asking and listening' with her fingertips and she 'hears' life and gets 'answers'. At this point we exceed the limits of our existing cultural codes. The phenomena cannot be translated into words for lack of concepts.

As L.J. cannot find suitable concepts, she has to use metaphors. She transfers a concept from a reality and context that we know: for example, she links the concept or code, 'to listen and hear' with the ears, to another context, 'to listen' with the fingertips. Because the word is transferred to another position, or set in another context, it receives a new meaning.

All new reality has to be grasped in this way, by the use of metaphors; pioneers, in particular, are forced to use them. Metaphors give new associations that help us grasp new realities.

This is the way culture is created, and it is created constantly. Much 'reality' has not yet been arranged, it has not yet been classified or given concepts.

When L.J. is 'listening with her fingertips and hears what is alive or dead', she is giving old words new associations and new meanings, different from those we already know.

She is one of the few, if not the only one, who is trying to approach the human being, the living, the potentially living and the dead in it, without trying to knit together 'truths' from natural sciences and Freud. As a pioneer she has to use metaphors as tools in order to communicate.

She has an approach which is original and an understanding of the human being for which we do not have concepts, and she is using herself in the therapeutic process on a level which physiotherapists usually have not experienced.

That is why her therapy and knowledge are a source of inspiration to those who try to move on and away from the old dusty concepts.

INTRODUCTION

Integrated Respiration* Therapy (IRT) is a therapy combining a psychoanalytic orientation including dream material, free association and expression in the form of rhymes, rigmaroles and songs.

IRT is founded on a concept of the healthy person and attempts to present an integrated approach to the understanding of the mind/body* relationship.

The theory behind the therapy is that the healthy human being is one who has passed through all the development stages without being infringed or inhibited. In such beings the entire body — not just the lungs — is breathing.*

Through treatment and observation of hundreds of patients, and use of the muscular-respiratory diagnosis scheme, I have developed the IRT theory and therapy.

Individual growth/human development goes through several stages of development and involves two assumed characteristics: (1) it takes place in the fullness of time*, and (2) it takes place on the terms of the individual himself.

Repressed material of mind and body will in return locate in particular zones corresponding to the unfulfilled stage in development. These zones will be hypotonic* with underdeveloped musculature*. They can be discovered and evaluated and charted so that they form the basis for diagnosis and prognosis.

The therapy is based on a colour protocol — an evaluation of psycho/physical resources which I have called the muscular-respiratory diagnosis scheme. To the therapist it is a remedy to help her establish a structured and safe course towards better health for the patient.

The evaluation and treatment involve a light touch to various areas of the body. This touch cannot be compared with massage or other muscle manipulation.

The hands and fingertips are of great importance. Through the light touch, using the fingertips, it is possible to feel the consistency of hypotonic and hypertonic* musculature.

If the contact I make with the body through my 'asking' hand is correct in terms of its preconscious state, position and function, and is timely and appropriate in its quality, then the person will respond as if 'speaking' and will 'answer'. It will be felt as something familiar, something which 'concerns' him and he will give those forms of expression mentioned above.

The treatment takes place in silence. Silence is an important

*There is a definition for every term which is asterisked in the appendix at the end of the chapter.

part of the reintegrating process. Therefore all disturbing noise from the surroundings has to be avoided.

The person will respond through changing respiratory patterns, various emotions and an urge to talk. Often the person begins to recover lost memories from the remote past. This means that the person's reactions will tell me what to do.

The way in which the hand really works can only be made comprehensible through IRT training. More written details could easily bring about misunderstandings and misuse. You cannot be a pianist only by reading notes.

I emphasize this because IRT does *not* concentrate on tense muscles, the person's defence mechanism, but on the hypotonic or underdeveloped muscular qualities. I do not think in muscles but in breathing. In other words, my theory and therapy is concerned with the positive resources in the individual, and the underlying theory is the healthy human being as an integrated, healthy and joyous individual — 'the breathing me'.

HISTORICAL BACKGROUND

I have developed my theory and therapy through my work with psychiatric patients whom I examined and treated in hospitals and in private practice. The patients' disturbances ranged from mild to more serious neuroses and psychoses, with an emphasis on seriously neurotic states.

When I started my work with these patients in the late 40s, physiotherapy was only beginning to be practised in mental hospitals. It was the Norwegian physiotherapist Aadel-Bülow-Hansen who introduced physiotherapy to psychiatric patients. At first it involved a treatment of symptoms based on local somatic problems. Later on, treatment centred on nervous mechanisms, and the focus was upon tension and defence.

Through practice, however, I became especially absorbed by what I, at that time, called underdeveloped musculature, with regard to different qualities of consistency. In a psychological sense, my hypothesis was that muscular characteristics indicated disturbances in the steps of development and the patient's way of coping with them.

At this time this was my hypothesis, and I started to chart and compile records of symptoms: details of the muscular-respiratory conditions involved were rendered in different colours and shades on my chart (see Fig. 8.1).

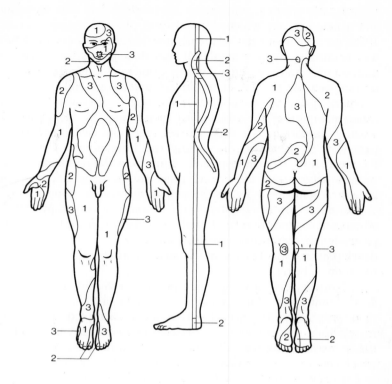

Diagnostic meaning of numbered areas

1 Green   Pre-functional muscle qualities, activated through respiration. Pre-conscious character structure.

2 Blue   Hypotonic muscle qualities, partially activated through respiration. Inactive character structure.

3 Red   Hypertonic muscle qualities with various degrees of tension, not activated through spontaneous respiration. Manifestations of voluntary respiration. Defence character structure.

Yellow   Smooth, slippery muscle qualities. Functionally unrelated to respiration. Defensive and non-genuine character structure.

Profile   Summarizes the key findings represented in the figures on the left and the right.

The colour of the straight line, in the centre figure, indicates the direction in which the conditioned reactions work and their developmental stage of settlement.
The colour of the backbone line indicates how the individual has further coped with his inauthentic self.

In normal practice this chart is coloured in by the therapist. The reader can obtain an impression of the result by colouring in the numbered areas according to the colours given against each number in the key.

Fig. 8.1 Muscular-respiratory diagnosis scheme (1950).

From this starting point my work resulted in a new paradigm and a new gateway which differed from physical therapy. In the 1950s my idea about the relationship of respiration to musculature was confirmed by my clients. It was during this time that the philosophy and wisdom which emerged during therapy overstepped the borders of traditional psychology and psychiatry.

I participated in the obligatory training courses which at that time were part of the educational programme for therapists. Of greatest importance to my further activities with psychiatric patients was, however, my joining the International Forum for Psychoanalysts and the inspiration I got from the psychiatrist Erik Fromm who asked me to continue my thinking about sound growth accompanied by its existential therapeutic approach.

Awareness of the Integrated Respiration Therapy (IRT) phenomenon, and its related methods, was not in evidence in the professional therapeutic world. There was at that time no developmental theory which focussed upon the ideal growth of the human being.

In Norway, my ideas and concepts were received and placed in an academic frame of understanding — on the basis of theory rather than practical experience. I immediately attempted to distance myself from this academic response to my work. My approach to the individual, however, did not conform to the prevalent science which focussed upon experimental work with my patients.

Then, eventually and unfortunately, this key phenomenon, the muscular-respiratory relationship, was adopted abroad, without attributing this key concept to an IRT source. This false adoption merely confirmed what Schopenhauer once said about new ideas. I will paraphrase his thought: 'To begin with, the individual rejected the idea, then took it for a given and, at last, handled it as her own.' The consequence was that IRT concepts were falsified and thrown into confusion, especially concepts connected with my idea about weak, underdeveloped muscles and their respiratory relationship. These principles were, and have been, misused by the body-oriented therapists. I am convinced, for instance, that the experience given through the reintegrating process of patients cannot be transferred into a bioenergetic framework or other modalities such as massage, acupressure, rolfing, etc. These programmed and directed approaches are not compatible with the IRT theory. Both in my country and elsewhere IRT concepts have been used in journals and books without an understanding of these core concepts.

My colour-protocol, or scientific map-work, became the gateway for IRT theory and is called muscular-respiratory diagnosis (MRD).

The theory is based on data obtained from approximately 200 patients examined and treated in hospitals and private practice (1946–66).

In addition, I have obtained data from educated students and students who attended my workshops abroad. Included in this material are about 150 tape-recordings†. They show how patients confirm my theory, especially through the word/sound phenomena which emerged over and over again in rhythm, rhymes, jingles and songs. As regards theory, the sound and word phenomena are systematically explained in my book about IRT theory/therapy (Johnsen, 1981).

In order to avoid misunderstandings between IRT and the many body-oriented therapies practised today, it is important to delineate some basic differences. (These differences, which became the IRT theory, receive clarification later in this chapter.) At its foundation, IRT has an existential framework which emerges out of a philosophy that the child must be evaluated in growth. Developmental growth centres* and growth elements* must be stimulated and psychophysically reintegrated. Reintegration for the individual takes place through metaphorical language, rhythms and song. From the therapist's standpoint, real integration* takes place in silence; the deepest harmony of silence is an experience beyond words. The stimulation in IRT is not physical manipulation but body listening. The essence of body listening means an ear—fingertip interaction, a listening—touch corroboration of latent resources. This, ultimately, means *interaction* rather than stimulation.

IRT cannot be classified as body-oriented therapy. In my conception, therapies that are body oriented are mainly concerned with muscle tension and defence mechanisms. Tension and defences in these therapies are treated as the gateway through which the therapist finds his bearing. In my view, then, therapy very easily functions on the terms of the therapist. IRT is a break with this approach.

The point of departure and the therapeutic process are so dissimilar to traditional methods that IRT has to be seen as an

---

†The recordings were taken during the treatment and with the acceptance of the patient. The recordings did not interfere with the treatment of the patient.

alternative or counterpart to physiotherapy. In Ancient Greek culture, body and breathing were one and the same thing; body and mind could not be separated. The intention of Integrated Respiration Therapy is the same.

I am aware that to talk about this method is antithetical to its essence; it must be experienced, and the true authenticity of this experience cannot be explained.

The therapist's observation about what is going on in the patient is not the same as the patient's own experience. This is the reason why in this chapter I describe the phenomena of IRT theory and therapy as established facts. I will ask you to bear the above mentioned in mind when going further into the subject. The discussion that follows attempts to state prosaically what is experienced poetically.

This brief historical background of my work, and my struggle to explicate it within the current physiological and psychological milieus, is given in the hope that it will provide some basic perspective for you as you continue to read about the concepts and theories of Integrated Respiration Therapy.

THE INTRAUTERINE WORLD AND BIRTH

The life of the fetus is not simply a time of physiological growth. The ocean the fetus dwells in is influenced by the mother's emotional and physiological state, just as the baby receives nutrients and hormone products through the umbilical cord. The rhythmic world that the baby lives in is perhaps of even greater importance. The mother's breathing is continual and affects her heartbeat. Her breathing can be deep, even and harmonious, reassuringly rhythmic and safe, reflecting a regular cycle of activity, rest and sleep. At the other extreme, the fetus is subject to constantly changing pressure in the abdominal cavity because of the digestive and respiratory tensions of the mother. At worst, there can be repeated uterine contractions, as in a threatened abortion, where the baby experiences the womb's painful attempts to eject it. An anxiety-ridden mother influences her child with constantly changing emotional states, with staccato, accelerated breathing, often followed by outbursts of weeping, increased abdominal pressure, great variations in heartbeat, irregular external activity, an absence of regular rest and sleep, together with a physiological effect due to an increase of stress hormones.

In response, the fetus reacts by increasing its activity; it responds with motoric restlessness. These sensations either become meaningful to the mother and eventually lead her to alter her frenetic activity, or she might recognize the influence of her tensions on the baby, feel guilty about them, but fall into helpless resignation at her inability to soothe her own rhythms and create the comforting environment she wants for her growing fetus.

The main point here is that even during the fetal stage there is an emotional relationship between mother and child which has its tangible expression. Mother and child actually communicate with each other and the first seeds of a mutual relationship are sown here. This relationship grows in dimension and significance as the time of birth draws near.

What sets birth in process is still a controversial medical question. I do not think we will find an answer to it by examining hormone concentrations or by using other mechanistic measurements. From a psychodynamic perspective, I am forced to conclude that birth is not a passive act of expulsion, but also implies an activity and a crucial experience on the part of the child. There is a parallel in the birth process to the phenomena of reintegration of a formerly traumatized patient's therapy, as we shall see. The patient senses 'something' he takes along with him — not only in the actual experience of 'rebirth', but also in his new experience of the original *growth centres* of formerly lost steps of development.† This is a world of signals, where a signal from the innermost heart sets the whole process in motion. This is consistent with the assertion that, in relation to other parts of the body, the heart is fully developed at birth. The theory of development including the ten different stages is described in my book *Birth and Rebirth in the Fullness of Time*.

The self is already initiated in the prenatal stage. It is autonomous even then. We have only to rediscover it. The growth elements for harmony are present and are meant to ensure that the baby is not born before its self feels the time is right, so that *the birth becomes a challenge it assumes on its own terms*.

The concept of the child as an autonomous being 'in the fullness of time' is substantiated by the large number of patients who have

†I have called the zones where growth actually manifests itself, *growth centres*. I describe the functions undergoing formation and differentiation which are ready for integration on the next level in terms of *growth elements*. And within the *growth elements*, always operating as the originating point for all emanations of impulse and expression, are the *nuclear phenomena*★ which are the decisive and critical points of reference during growth.

re-experienced their own birth under therapy. These patients experienced being reborn on their own terms, whereas at their 'original' infant births there were various reasons for the birth having been induced which had consequences in later stages of development. Damage occurred because the child's capacity to respect his own activity signals was not intact. Thus, it is the mother's and, in many cases the obstetrician's cooperation with the child's activity which is crucial here, and of importance also for the child's later, goal-directed actions. These actions come from the child's inherited autonomy which the child experiences as the definite truth.

In order to illustrate one reaction to birth, I will relate the following description as written to me by a patient who experienced her birth during Integrated Respiration Therapy.

Twenty-five-year-old woman (eighth treatment):

It seemed as if I had just lain down on my back and I was looking up at the usual spot in the ceiling and wondering what would happen today. After a short while I turned on my left side and pulled up my legs, bent my arms, and clenched my fists and lay all tucked up. As I was resting like this, gradually I felt an increasing need to pull my body more and more together. I strained to get my feet as tightly up under me as I felt I needed to, then I pulled to get my chin tucked completely into my chest. I could hardly breathe, but the need to be folded up was so strong that I had to do it. I closed my eyes tightly, to get darkness.

Now I felt an enormous pressure over my thighs. It came spasmodically. I turned around, still folded up, in order to have the weight resting on my left shoulder and forehead. As my chin hit the couch, my head went backwards, and I strove forwards, and suddenly my body unfolded, as if I were being stretched, and I grasped out with my left arm in order to get hold of something, and I lay with my face on one side and cried and laughed at once. Now I could breathe. A short while later I said 'I am so happy'. I felt incredibly alert, energetic and surrounded by lots of light and air — room to move. *Now I knew how it felt to be born. I was convinced — this is how my birth had been*: the effort till the goal was suddenly reached, and then the sudden unfolding. How shall I describe it: like racing through something incredibly soft, and a sensation of falling surrounded by red light and a sensation of lightness, space and air.

A few weeks later this experience repeated itself. But this time there was no pressure over my thigh. My right foot took over, and I made my way out; and, suddenly, there was a shout as if from my foot, an altogether exultant shout, and the lightness of my body was so much the stronger, the effortlessness. And the sensation of space and air — I can feel as clearly even today.

Our long childhood begins with the *nuclear phenomenon, the cry* — the first challenge, the first manifestation of oneself as an autonomous being. Breathing starts. As on the first day of creation, darkness becomes a sea of light. Water is exchanged for air. Air has its counterpart in the human organism. These two extremes are joined by the breath, which is transformed into a sound wave, and the long silence becomes sound in a cry of triumph. This experience brings the first moment of joy, coming on the strength of the anticipatory prefunctional content.* The self's growth centre at this stage is finished and stands ready for further challenges, while the growth elements are ready for further development. Joy has been manifested by a rhythmic sound, a wave of strength. This is the basis for one's tonal individuality in later development, and at the same time represents its confirmation. This very *first manifestation of one's self* (preceding the next level of a give-and-take relationship with the mother) *occurs through sound. This must be emphasized if one is to understand the developmental process and the significance therapy gives to all primal forms of sound expression. The sound system of the individual is a universal language having fundamental significance for later expression of the self, and it is established at this stage.* The sounding board is established to confirm and provide resonance for the sound phenomena of subsequent development stages. Moreover, the motto is set in the psychic body for natural growth towards new challenges. The triumphant feeling experienced here of once having commanded a full-toned expression is remembered as support in later dealings with difficult situations that might tempt us to hedge from an outspoken sound system.

At the second stage of development, the most clearly apparent *growth centre*, the throat/palate, develops out of a basic impulse coming from the *diaphragm*. Under the assumption that the *growth centre is prefunctional*, that is, ready for an expression of self-confirmation via the cry, this growth centre will be accomplished by manifestation of the cry, and will be integrated via respiration into the spontaneous breathing.

At birth, the main activity impulse in the child seems to stem from the *viscera* (the heart, lungs, liver, kidneys, intestines, etc.) *to the foot.* From here, the impulse travels simultaneously to the *os sacrum*, with the 'tail' as steering mechanism, cooperating with the *heel/ankle* in a rhythmic wave movement which prompts the baby to push its way out, to 'crawl out' on its own terms. This reintegrated process shows that this basic activity factor determines the child's first growth to independent action and fulfillment of his first challenge in the external world. *The completeness of the breathing and the cry depend on the extent to which the activity impulse from the pelvis and heel are followed up, or how the impulses are influenced by outer elements.*

Here is a quotation which illustrates sound and tone and their relationship to the signal for activity in the foot.

The tone strikes into me
The tone is the whole mouth
The tone mouths out into the now, mouths out within me
The tone is a lovely unity in my head and in my foot
Tone's sound and tone's root.
Tone, tone is the journey, tone, tone, foot and foot . . . .

The collective impulses from the pelvis and heel will be absent when the birth situation has had interference. The baby's cry and manifestation of breathing will not be fully accomplished. The foundation for the child's full self-confirmation will have already suffered a set-back.

BASIC PHENOMENA OF THE 'BREATHING ME'

The healthy person is seen as one who has passed through and *experienced with joy* all mind/body developmental stages. No external forces have infringed or inhibited the organism's inner pulsation, its experience of growth, and the opportunity of discovering new developmental attitudes and responses which move toward the expansion of the total range of human potential and expression.

The healthy personality is able to breathe deeply using his whole body, instead of breathing while using only the accepted breathing musculature (intercostal, diaphragmatic and adjoining throat musculature). The whole of the body musculature is utilized in the establishment of a living, breathing, flowing, rhythmic whole. The expressive language of such whole-body breathing is characterized by its tone, wave, life energy and strength. In the healthy body these characteristics function harmoniously and one can say that the body is 'in tune' — vibrating on one continuous axis from the finger muscles to the toe muscles, and encompassing the whole of the body as the wave passes along it. This is what I like to call the '*breathing me*.'

There is hidden poetry within the body and the 'breathing me' is the vehicle with which these lost but not dead creative resources* can be brought to the surface, with expression. As I have mentioned, this new potential in the patient is often revealed spontaneously through the expressive content of rhymes, poems and rituals. Through these, *the positive primitive world which is seated in the patient takes on form and is experienced with joy and wonderment*. It is a joy which represents something fundamental and almost immutable in the life process; a joy through which emotions 'reach out' in a 'true to one's self' form of expression. In this connection I cannot emphasize enough the importance of bringing the growing elements of happiness to the foreground: those elements usually found hidden in the locked-off expectant content of respiration. Expression of this 'true to one's self' language is often hampered, especially in the developing child. This is done by the disintegrating and disorientating effect of structured learning, which blocks the fluency and integrating effect of the growing elements contained in rhymes, sounds, jingles and songs.

Intervention during this important process interferes with the focussing of the child's natural philosophy. The child internalizes rhymes and verses and songs in order to bring about and strengthen mind/body harmony. By using sounds and rhymes patients manage to sing themselves into insight, putting their words and feelings into verse:

I am me and you are you,
Yes, I am me and you are you
Because when I am me and you are you
We can really be happy about each other.†

This expressive language of such whole-body breathing allows joy to spread. Joy is the real source of the human being. It is joy in the children's songs, play and dance. It is joy we know as adults when we perceive our positive signals or surrender to rhythm from the external world.

On the way towards the ideal goal of spontaneous and integrated respiration, one patient expressed himself with rhythmical

---

†This is a tape recorded quotation from a therapy situation.

emphasis. He shifted to speak in English, although Danish was his native language:

The gravity of moods around me,
Breathing them in and out
I feel what happened so clear,
When atmosphere of fear comes near
I find something else to do.
I cannot breathe in fear.
Why not — why don't I dare?
Its gravity is too great and I feel so weak and tender,
The gravity of fear is as great as gravity of safety
So now I know what happened to my safety:
I never was allowed to feel the genuine fear,
And now I dare to feel the fear
So now it always disappears — leaving me safe.

With the newly attained experience of safety, the patient who made up this poem took the final step into full responsibility for himself.

Using my patients' recorded words, I have illustrated how people in therapy began to experience body/mind areas that had not been developed, and then they reintegrated them into their mind and body. This material naturally varies from individual to individual, but it also bears striking similarities. By repeated evidence we are brought to the conclusion that a universal creative ability lies latent in the child during early phases of development. This creative element is associated with the cosmos, with a deeper common source, older than religion, which gives the patients' utterances a ritual character.

Figure 8.2 illustrates the ideal conditions of the 'breathing me'. The basic terms presented here might give some insight into the complexity, and innate simplicity, of this theory and therapy.

Originally, the individual possesses a universal harmony and balance*, which is the inherent code of each person. This inherent code can be seen as the predestined stages of development, pertaining to all of us. However, few people develop under completely beneficial circumstances or receive the confirmations needed at each developmental step. This ideal state of existence also presupposes a personal commitment to the values of one's cultural heritage.

In straightforward terms, the healthy person can be characterized as the one who has the opportunity to develop in accordance with his inherent code, when growth centres have been

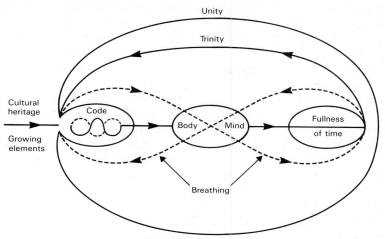

Fig. 8.2 Integrated respiration therapy.
The code. Growth elements: the genuine and autonomic element from which the individual derives impulses and gets signals of action. The genuine phylogenetic and ontogenetic heritage.
Body/mind. Phenomenology: experience of the self as a monologue between the genuine signals and the body — the child's intrinsic world.
Fullness of time. Nuclear phenomenon: the existential aspect, showing the importance of the ability to master new challenges when the child is mature enough, neither earlier nor later.

accomplished in the fullness of time. Ideally, we can speak of a trinity:

inherent code——+ body/mind——+ fullness of time (see Fig. 8.2)

In the fullness of time the inherent code drives the child towards mastering new challenges, presupposing a fearless, free breathing. Then the child is ready for birth, ready for crawling, ready for standing, and ready for integrated understanding of words, etc. The greatest and most penetrating experience of joy is to master 'standing on our own feet', and the experience of genuine understanding of words.

Code, body/mind and fullness of time eventuate in an integrated new level of existence. The therapist keeps this trinity in mind and takes care to observe non-interference during the process, and remain a mere shadow in the background. At all costs, the breathing wave of the patient is not to be disturbed. The point is that through growth the balance of the trinity is very easily disturbed, especially at those times when the child is ready to incur new growth centres. If the balance becomes threatened just then, all one's strength is devoted to restoring it again. If this does not work, disintegration of body/mind takes place and fear takes hold. Interference from the outside world brings a split into the breathing wave.

Only when the anticipatory content of disturbed areas is stimulated and reawakened will the weakened part be taken into the whole and reintegrated. A chain-reaction follows, mobilizing still more parts of anticipatory potentials. Harmony is re-established in one's being, peace is regained.

The person who, thus, is at one with himself and knows who he is, will, as a natural consequence of his uniqueness, recognize the 'other'. For each *individual*, for each person who has found harmony, balance and health, it is obvious that 'I am me, you are you'. When one is healthy, one respects another's identity and does not intrude upon it.

THE PSYCHOPHYSICAL PROCESS: A HYPOTONIC-RESPIRATION RELATIONSHIP

It had been assumed by therapists, influenced by the work of Wilhelm Reich (1949), and later by others, that until the body armour or tense musculature was relaxed there could be no spontaneous activity or experience, and therefore no new psychological development. But I found that the underlying repressed experiences were not automatically released when muscular tensions were removed. In fact, concentration on muscular mental defences via the relaxation of muscular tension often resulted in a weakening of psychophysical integration. Patients subsequently reported having experienced anxieties and depressions which they never had before. Such patients may have been deprived of defences that supported them. It is often considered a sign that repression remains as long as the body stays rigid, but this in itself is not a good basis on which to plan treatment. Tension and defence are not a starting point — the basis should be the hidden and forgotten tendencies of expression.

An essential link in the total psycho-body structure which has been overlooked in other therapies is the weak (hypotonic) muscular state. According to the hypothesis that physical aspects correspond to the psychological stage of the patient, a first step for me was to differentiate between the various muscle qualities.*

The distinction is one not only between tense and normally relaxed muscles, but also between the latter and weak, 'underdeveloped' muscles. The distinction is not only important as such, but is also of primary importance to the treatment of patients with a mild degree of pathology.

With tensions, the psycho-body structure can become both stiff (hypertonic) and paralysed with anxiety. Inhibited emotion and repressed memories are expressed in the hypotonic musculature through constrained respiration and various degrees of resignation or surrender. These body factors serve to limit spontaneity. On the basis of the verbal and respiratory responses of my patients whose hypotonic muscles have been stimulated, it has been my impression that the different hypotonic degrees found in the body are indicative of various latent emotional potentials. By shifting the emphasis from hypertonic to hypotonic muscles, the aim, as well as the results, of treatment are changed. Tensions subside and disappear as the repressed experiences are recalled and assimilated. This occurs without a direct concentration on the defences.

Let us now look at the term 'hypotonic musculature'. The hypotonic muscular consistency* gives the impression of being 'limp' but is of an altogether different character from ordinary relaxed muscles with normal tonus. The limpness which marks hypotonic muscles is a limp consistency with a dystonic character, coupled with a yielding tonus. There are several degrees of limpness, which indicate that the muscles have different qualities of consistency. The overall impression is one of limpness concurrent with a varied 'content' of immanent potential (energy), different degrees and forms of non-realized activity. Owing to the general complexion, the limp consistency, this energy has no possibility of realization. It is not easy to find adequate expressions for the different shades of content. This is not due to the palpable qualities, but to the fact that terminology is not sufficiently differentiated to describe either the muscular qualities or the psychological implications involved. To describe hypotonic musculature it is necessary to realize one thing, which from the very beginning I found easy to demonstrate. On handling aspects of hypotonic muscles one always obtains variable respiratory responses. Literature contains descriptions of respiratory conditions, but does not formulate the relationship between musculature and respiration. No such respiratory response is obtained when handling tense musculature. The functional relationship between hypotonic activation and respiration will be described later. Judging from my experience, respiration is of central importance, not only for the method of treatment, but also in diagnostic appraisals and prognostications.

The consistency which primarily attracted my attention, precisely because of its marked respiratory response, was the quality covered by the term, 'mobilizable expective content'.†

1. Limp hypotony (pre-conditioned): 1 in Figure 8.3.

The muscles show a weak consistency, but have in them elements of firmness. It is this factor of consistency which characterizes the quality. The muscles seem to reveal strong elements of latent forces, an activity of expectancy. The quality is appreciable and mobilizable.

A therapist with little experience or lacking sensitivity in her fingers, may easily mistake the extent of expectancy for normally relaxed muscle if she is not aware of how the respiratory conditions are incorporated into the muscle qualities. Muscular stimulation results in direct inspiration and expiration which is complete and often followed by a distinct change in tonus. The weak hypotone quality is replaced by an even consistency, the normal relaxed one. It is this kind of hypotone muscle which I consider important for the planning and implementation of constructive treatment.

2. Feeble hypotony (mobilizable): 2 in Figure 8.3

These muscles are of a weak nature, but show signs of a certain hidden firmness which gives the impression of limpness to the overall picture. The feeble muscular quality is appreciable and mobilizable. Latent forces are also present at this stage, but they are weaker and have less shape than in the previous case. The respiratory response is also instantaneous, but stops at the expiratory phase. A very slight difference in quality may be felt in the tonic conditions during inspiration and expiration. The feebleness of the muscles gives way to a somewhat firmer quality, but the expiration does not result in lasting or far-reaching change.

---

†Mobilizable means possible to mobilize. In other words the muscles are prefunctional, i.e. very near conscious awareness and mature enough to be stimulated and reintegrated.

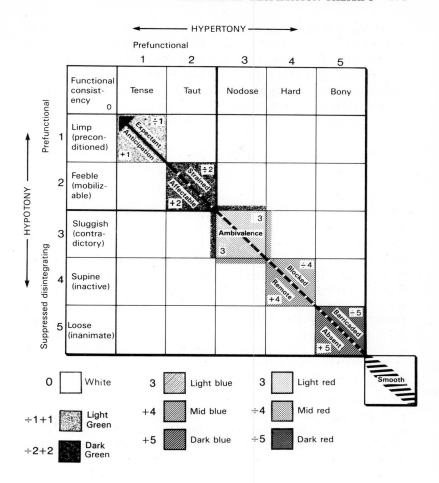

Fig. 8.3 By means of tonic conditions and respiratory response concerning hypotonic muscles, it is just possible to describe the functional state of the patient, physical as well as psychical. These correlates are shown by the diagonal.

3. *Sluggish hypotony* (contradictory): 3 in Figure 8.3

The consistency of the muscles is weak and contains characteristics of both response and withdrawal. The respiratory response is hesitant and delayed. The quality is sluggish and, on activation, has an equal possibility of advancing to 'feeble' as well as of acquiring a less active tendency. The quality is accessible, but should not, as a rule, be mobilized. Any possibility of mobilization depends upon the content of sluggish consistency. This may vary greatly from one case to another. The quality constitutes the individual form of ambivalence. The manifested behaviour and the resolution found differ from patient to patient. Similarly, the consistency may vary from a light, compact, sluggish consistency to a coarser, more leather-like or padded form, where the outer layer of muscle is somewhat separate from the tonus in the consistency as a whole.

4. Supine hypotony (affectively inactive): 4 in Figure 8.3

These muscles are also of a weak nature and present no sign of elasticity. Their nature is one of inactivity and dullness. No latent forces can be found and no respiratory reaction is experienced. The activation of the consistency will bring about further slackness. The respiratory response will follow the release of the grip on the muscle, now as inspiration. After a pause, the expiration will follow as a slight cough or similar expression of defence.

5. Loose hypotony (inanimate): 5 in Figure 8.3

The consistency of these muscles is exceptionally weak: they give the impression of slightness. The quality is one of lack of feature, i.e. inanimate and immobilizable. Also in this case, the respiration will follow the release of the grip, and now as a faint inspiration; no expiration may be detected.

As previously mentioned it is my impression that the hypotonic degrees indicate various emotional potentials. In the limp and feeble hypotonic conditions it is possible to mobilize emotionality. The muscles can, thus, be termed emotionally prefunctional. Stimulation of the limp hypotony results in an emotional ease and relief. This category of hypotony is accessible for reintegration. A stimulation of the feeble hypotony also results in an emotional mobilization, but will only on rare occasions lead to relief. The mobilization usually shows itself by various slight vegetative symptoms, or strained emotional forms of expression, dependent upon previous integration in therapy.

This becomes quite clear in the sluggish hypotony, the quality being of an indifferent nature, and indicates a subdued, diffuse firmness, giving an overall picture of inelasticity. Therefore these qualities cannot be treated by direct approach.

As to muscular testing, the respiratory phenomena is not so easily observable. Fingertip sensibility of the therapist is of great importance, especially concerning limp hypotony.

EVALUATION OF RESOURCES BASED ON THE TOTAL STRUCTURAL AND DYNAMIC CONDITION

The aims of treatment are to find positive ways to encourage the resources of the patient. I believe that the stimulation of hypotonic muscles is the basis for extended experience and personal integration in the individual. When the concealed content of hypotonia is brought forth during treatment, realization and integration take place and the state of respiratory failure abates. The hypotonic qualities become normal and tensions give way. Through stimulation of the hypotonic muscles there is a respiratory response manifested by a slight difference in quality of expiration and inspiration. This reveals the patient's resources and the potentials which may be mobilized. The relationship of tonus to the respiratory answer indicates how profoundly the personality has been made impenetrable.

The hypotonic prefunctional qualities and the respiratory response indicate in which phase the respiration has been repressed. By comparing muscle qualities with respiration it will become apparent which aspects of respiration are spontaneous and which are held back. The pauses (the 'keeping back') in the respiratory phase vary: from pause between *in* and *ex*piration or between *ex* and *in*spiration, to restraint of the final phase of inspiration or the final phase of expiration. This line of thought is illustrated in Figure 8.4. This is the crucial understanding of the process.

When resources in the hypotonic muscles are mobilized, a release in the restraint of the respiration will follow, influencing the muscular relationship and giving the tense musculature normal consistency. The activation leads to integration and to a global functional effect, so that motor expression, experience and respiration function together. The healthy spontaneity in the structure of bodily carriage presupposes the pattern shown in Figure 8.4. The process depends on the degree of uniformity of the muscular quality between different aspects of growth. This,

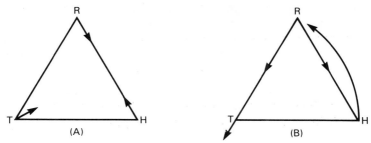

Fig. 8.4   The blocked form of the relationship between tension, hypotonia and respiration symbolically represented: T = tension; H = hypotonia; R = respiration.

Figure 8.4 (A) demonstrates a blocked form, where the hypotonia continues, the respiration is not released and the tensions are being maintained. One could imagine this as a set of forces tied together and resulting in a rigid fixation. If the patient has resources that could be mobilized this might be illustrated in figure 8.4 (B): relationship between tension, hypotonia and respiration when hypotonic muscles are being mobilized.

together with the respiratory conditions, may lead to an appraisement of responses which the patient can mobilize. This can also indicate the treatment to be followed.

In one sense the nature of underdeveloped musculature is one of lack of expression, and in another, one of resources not yet mobilized. The individual differences in total resources for expression will be found. The relationship between T, H and R in Figure 8.4 will tell whether the total structure has been blocked by a traumatic experience or by defensive identification, or possibly by some other personality-restraining mechanism. Still, irrespective of causality, the resources of the total structure will show the possibility of emotional experience and the nature of the content which, through adequate treatment, can be given significant expression. The resource factors in the total structure may also give a hint of the patient's possibilities for treatment, even where psychodiagnostics indicate the possibilities of treatment to be slight.

Finally, I have indicated a graphic demonstration of different types of respiratory response (see Fig. 8.5) as another clue in the patient's evaluation. Understanding the patient's breathing wave is paramount to knowing the steps to follow in the treatment. Stimulation of specific body areas is governed by the therapist's sensitivity to seeing and feeling the respiratory response. The individual's structural and psychic condition is revealed and evaluated through the diagnostic recognition of changing

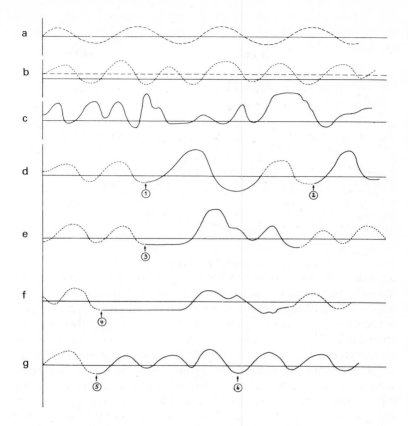

Fig. 8.5   Graphic demonstration of different types of waves of respiratory response.

Graph A: shows the calm, even, harmonious breathing of a well-integrated person.

Graph B: illustrates the 'normal', average respiration pattern found in relatively well-compensated neurotics. The pattern shows a slightly increased rate, slight irregularity in the depths, as well as a tendency towards holding back full expiration, with incomplete deep inhalation.

Graph C: indicates respiration in an openly anxious state. It is quickened to a staccato, with gasping inhalation, held at intervals, in a chaotic pattern.

Graphs D, E, F, G: give a visual picture of waves of respiratory response after stimulation. Indications 1 and 2 point to stimulation of prefunctual musculature; 3 indicates musculature with positive ambivalence; 4 shows musculature conveying the quality of hypotonic resignation. On the tense side, responsive musculature corresponds to 5 and 6.

respiratory responses. The types of response, as indicated in Figure 8.5, follow the stimulation of individual resources. The graph shows different types of respiratory patterns as they move within the body.

INTEGRATED RESPIRATION THERAPY: A RESOURCE ORIENTED APPROACH

What we must take extreme care to do is to assess the extent to which the individual has defended his organism during this preverbal state, the extent to which a false ego has invaded the personality. This is the unique pattern of respiratory adjustment which the individual has adopted. In short, we must know where and what our patient's resources are, and how deeply embedded they are. Our aim in therapy is to bring these deep-seated personal needs *safely to the surface* in a way which allows them to become fully integrated into the personality.

Integrated respiration therapy is *essentially* a resource-oriented approach. It releases and activates latent aspects of personality through physical experience. Preverbal inhibitions often represent the fundamental inhibitions which impair personality development. I have found that it is particularly difficult to reach and treat this level of repressed experience if there is an exclusive verbal emphasis in therapy. In IRT, other kinds of expression are promoted through physical stimulation, and the resulting experiences are then integrated through memory. In other words, I have discovered that ear/fingertip listening of the anticipatory content in the muscular structure results in random verbal associations, meaningful dream material, and spontaneous body reaction, as well as a gradual release of restrained respiration.

IRT, like many other therapies, centres on a nucleus of neurotic structure which is specific for each individual. But therapies with strictly intellectually-based insights may only succeed in achieving a limited improvement, or, at best, an adjustment to neurotic conflict. Even though a patient has intellectual insight into his early experiences, constructive new behaviour and feelings may be difficult to attain if there is no spontaneous physical activity. A resource-oriented approach results in progressively deeper layers of repressed experience reaching a higher level of consciousness and becoming integrated. Integration takes place in the body and the mind simultaneously as respiration moves symbolically, step by step into the different 'rooms of one's house'.

The healthy person is able to maintain a harmonious interplay between all elements of the body from internal organs to superficial muscle layers. Integrated Respiration Therapy sees the preconscious hypotonic musculature as the key to the hidden latent resources of the individual. In this musculature lies the core of the individual's resources. When activated, these resources contain the missing link to spontaneous respiration. They represent the locked off emotional expression that is now a mobilizable 'expectant' content which has been hidden by the lack of integrated respiration.

Fundamentally, the essence of IRT is not a question of musculature as such. It is a question of bringing forth hidden emotions (resources) to be experienced and worked through for the benefit of ongoing life. It becomes an issue concerning the ability of the body to distribute the mobilizable 'expective' content economically and efficiently throughout the whole organism.

In the final analysis, IRT's approach is to recognize that the resource which lies at the core of every human being is joy. The body/mind must become attuned and tuned in to the inner melody before song can be expressed. The patient's tune, his true self, can be detected in his respiratory patterns. Ultimately, this therapy is after a melody played by the body in a rhythmic revelation, so that each individual has his *own* melody, his own tune — an absolute resourceful song of life!

MUSCULAR RESPIRATION DIAGNOSIS: PLOTTING A PATIENT'S RESOURCES

Muscular respiratory diagnosis (MRD) tells us which parts of the body require physical stimulation. Diagnosis reveals which part of the body should be given priority, and through external stimulation of that area intra-physical impulses are generated. These impulses may 'rise to the surface' or reflect themselves in the form of direct verbal association, bodily activity and, most importantly, dream material.

The therapist must find a system that helps plot a patient's resources. I will not go into detail about all of my ways of conducting MRD but will offer some general observations and suggestions. The therapy itself is based on a diagnosis of the respiratory quality of body musculature. As we already know, the muscular quality of the body reflects the influences of the emotional conflict in the organism. MRD studies and assesses the different levels at which full respiration has been blocked. Variations in consistency and quality in the muscular-respiration relationship are plotted in the patient's profile. Such a schematic charting can serve as an indicator to the therapist of the patient's inner resources and developmental possibilities. The spectrum of such a profile is illustrated in Figure 8.3. There are five categories in this Figure, each of which requires a distinct therapeutic approach. The graph represents the dynamic potential which the therapist can use as a visual identification of the patient and can, subsequently, chart as an initial 'diagnostic' evaluation for that patient.

I found, early on, that a symbolic colour scheme was useful when doing MRD. The relationship of the colours to the muscle consistency and character attitude is, indeed, a symbolic one. During a muscular-respiratory examination, the total picture of muscular consistency and quality are charted in relationship to respiration. In order to simplify the structural picture, one can fill in the evaluation of muscle consistency in colours on a special 'muscular-respiratory diagnosis scheme' (Fig. 8.1). In charting patients, one can get a complete picture of a person's 'pattern' with the use of these colours. I cannot emphasize strongly enough the significance of the colour pattern, the interplay of resources, which serve as an evaluation of the body's mobilizable muscular areas.

As I have stated in this chapter, from an examination of the respiratory quality of body musculature we can calculate the resources of the patient, that is his capacity for becoming healthy. At the same time we can construct a working picture or pattern of the psychodynamic affect of anxiety and conflict on the mind/body complex. I have found that through MRD the *preconscious character structure* (which in somatic terms is represented by prefunctional qualities) holds the key to our understanding of the patient's psychophysical picture, and provides us with the best opportunity for plotting a *structured and safe* course towards real health.

IRT: AN INTERACTION OF HAND AND DREAM

I do not know with certainty what the hand conveys, or why it is such an effective and powerful medium. But it is a certainty that the hand is a key phenomenon in integration. The therapist uses his hand in IRT as a medium to build a bridge to the patient's resources and to his individuality which was lost perhaps during development. In everyday life, as well, the hand is significant in many ways: some people talk with their hands to emphasize meaning; one shakes hands, places a hand on another's shoulder, or head, or takes another by the hand. All of this reflects sympathy, expresses trust between people, or is at least a means of expression that reveals feeling. Today, too, we talk of good hands, of healing hands.

From earliest times, the hand has been associated with religious rituals, magic and miraculous healings. By 'laying on of hands' people made medicine unnecessary when it was done by a person with 'healing powers'. In IRT it is *one's own breathing that heals, as the hand touches.*

In practical terms when this physical stimulation is indicated during treatment, I work with those areas closest to surface awareness. If the part of the body which I stimulate is correct in terms of its preconscious state, position and function, and is timely and appropriate in its quality, then the body and mind will respond as if 'speaking' and will 'answer'. The contact will be felt by the patient as something familiar, something which concerns him, something enabling him to make a response, to project the content of the hampered feelings through psychophysical means.

The hand awakens to life the growth elements not reached by the breathing wave; it releases a process which the patient attempts to integrate. The touch is gentle, like the hand that takes hold of the baby's head as it is born. The hand is friendly, sensitive, suited to welcoming new life, adaptable, secure and safe. At the same time it has a certain expectancy in its touch, a plea that says: 'Come on, now, what do you really want? Let's have a look at you; you went and hid yourself once but now there's no more danger.' It is as if the touch calls out to the individual's resources. Almost nothing is said; all is implicit in the touch, sure but delicate, tender yet objective.

Sometimes I may speak briefly, to interrupt the patient's protective mechanism when I see that he or she is on the edge of expression. What I say then becomes an 'inner voice' for the patient; he takes it along with him and may give it expression silently, verbally or physically.

Most of the time I am silent, while my hand is listening. In this way I can avoid influencing the sensitivity of the content under development. When my hand is in touch with the patient's body, my silence is not felt as aloofness. The hand's soft, enveloping touch stimulates the growth element. I wait for the body to reaffirm itself, to integrate its powers. I simply affirm the integration with my touch. The touch acknowledges the dynamics of the growth centre. The hand cares for, encircles, acknowledges and questions — depending on the nature of the dynamics present.

Stimulation by the hand usually occurs at a point which delicately anticipates the patient's readiness, and takes, as it were, its messages from an awareness of just when and where the patient's own signal is about to dawn. When the intrapsychic sensation has been awakened, the hand only acts as a reminder to keep the process going. In IRT the hand 'tunes in' and calls out what is latent within the person: the anticipatory prefunctional area. It is other-centred. When my hand stimulates, I feel that something is underway. Respiration makes a way for itself, the musculature revives, the respiratory wave establishes itself; the patient senses these phenomena and often breathes deeply simultaneously. It is like an interchange between body and breathing. In treatment, one's hand revives a new dimension as confirmation of the restraint that is being released. The effect is as if to vibrate the chord in the person's register of impulses that has been destroyed or damaged. In this way the hand stimulates the chord, step by step, so that the impulse from rhythm to sound is won back again.

The effect of the hand on one's dream state can either inhibit or stimulate. The therapist stimulates the dream material by helping to attune the patient's respiration. The missing expressive tendencies are stimulated and emerge gradually throughout the day, live with the patient, grow and synthesize into new wholes that are ultimately expressed in dream. It is then that the patient's own interpretations and associations become crucial. The patient may be surprised at his dreams and the real significance they now have for him. Instead of experiencing them from a distance as if in a cinema, dreams live on in him as something significant and personal, leading him towards greater self-knowledge and discovery, towards a truer acquaintance with his own inner life. It is the patient, with the help of the therapist, who can and must decipher the valuable information about problems and conflicts which now lie close to the surface, the indicators of ambivalence and its cause. Through dreams the incomprehensible, the unknown, is transformed into symbolic language that opens the way for a new dimension of the mind, since the protective mechanism of the ambivalence is translated into images that fantasy can grasp and understand.

There are two aspects to this symbolic language: firstly, it opens a new depth of consciousness, with metaphor as the gateway, and, secondly it shows the way into this new dimension. Together, these two aspects give a sense of one's self in terms of one's own symbolism. Dream images extend one's being, show the way to one's 'true self'. In the symbolic language of dreams, a feeling crystallizes an image which cannot be expressed in normal language, but which provides a key to understanding that which has not yet become one's ultimate being. The dream-dynamics give the patient this possibility. The atmosphere, pictures and dynamics of dreams are based on a corrective emotional experience in the patient and he will detect his 'true self' by means of a metaphorical language and the intensely personal atmosphere of his dreams. The patient forms a personal language of his own, thus expressing in a better way his inner activity and life. The metaphorical language thus spoken of is a penetrating reflection of the inner life of the patient.

While I do not employ traditional dream interpretation methods, I may put forward one or two questioning words through which the patient can work, unless the dream is one I refer to as a 'key dream', in which case I say nothing. My experience confirms that by using this resource-oriented approach, and its dream productivity, it is possible to tap latent resources and to utilize them in a drive towards re-establishing a balanced and integrated personality.

WHO CAN DO IRT?

It seems natural to ask: who can do IRT? An important point to emphasize is that IRT is not body therapy. It is a method based on a theory which is different as well as contrary to traditional body-oriented thinking.

Generally speaking, I like to train relatively healthy people who have not been trained in other methods before. The emotional/philosophical understanding, most often buried in the very first steps of development, is difficult to reach for those who have been trained traditionally/intellectually, e.g. vegetotherapists as well as orthodox psychoanalysts. In summary, I will train any integrated person who has kept his intuition, i.e. someone who has not been adapted to reversed thinking.

For anyone who has completed a professional clinical education in psychotherapy, the training would take approximately two years. Training is based on personal treatment and theoretical as well as practical learning. Most important is the therapist's knowledge of his own signal system, so that he can follow the reintegrating process taking place in the patient. Personal treatment is not a question of hours, but of integrity, which is demonstrated when the breathing wave is experienced as a penetrating source of existence and wholeness.

CONCLUDING STATEMENTS

It seems more difficult to investigate our own nature than the earth on which we live. Today we are so absorbed in the world outside ourselves that we forget or have completely lost sight of the signals from our inner world. We cannot regulate the universe, but we can regulate ourselves only by being attentive to our inner world of signals. This attentiveness goes far deeper than the intellect or feelings. It is the deepest kind of intuition in an understanding of one's own destiny, based on an understanding of one's being and the belief that actions based on the true self will win natural response in the outer world.

We are eternally searching for a solution to the problem of 'Who am I?' Integrated Respiration Therapy is another step, another possibility for solving that problem. It is a way to look at possibilities, those possibilities for that individual and for that structure; they are as infinite as Time. In this work, breathing is the deepest connection in your Being; it is both birth and rebirth. We are aware that breath is essential to life, but when breath and life are interrupted through inhibitory experiences, it seems essential that we investigate the resulting breath-related content. IRT is one way to do it.

It has been difficult to describe my work in words, to describe a process that is understood *only* through experience. Even at this advanced stage in the development of IRT, the linguistic context, the choice of words and the sentence structure can only give a hint of what is possible — and yet to be discovered in Integrated Respiration Therapy. It is my hope that the fundamental change in therapy, the tremendous feeling of something entirely new which you cannot label, is possible. All of us are after the desirable state of an integration of all our resources — synthesized into a functioning wholeness, realized in the 'fullness of time' — in the NOW. The search for the '*I Am Me*', in all of us, is a desirable goal. In fact, the dimensions of being human demand it!

APPENDIX: DEFINITION OF CONCEPTS IN IRT (In order of appearance)

Respiration

Respiration is the process by which IRT evaluates the body's performance. The therapist both observes the person visually and gently touches the body at selected points. By this means, the therapist can determine the extent to which the pulmonary function originating in the chest wall initiates movement, excitement and energy throughout the body. Pulmonary function and its expression throughout the organism can either express the integration of the body and personality by moving toward 'total breathing' or confirm the person's inability to be responsive to himself, others and his environment by freezing and immobilization.

Objectively in treatment, the visual and tactile examination of respiration indicates to the therapist the potential and yet unrealized resources of the person. Developmentally, respiration is the origin of growth and change. Therapeutically, respiration is a mediating mechanism whereby the body/mind shifts from the anxiety-ridden and problematic to the natural and spontaneous.

Breathing

Breathing, in Integrated Respiratory Therapy, refers to the capacity of the human body to integrate its entire experience in a single pulsation. Breathing is subjectively felt as the foundation of harmonious feelings. Objectively, it is the extension of the respiratory pattern throughout the entire organism. Breathing is not simply respiration in the support of physiological survival it is our avenue of resonance between our total being and the external world.

Fullness of time

A time segment of varying duration when the child (at each new step of growth) is permitted to gather its natural power, at its own pace.

Body and mind versus mind/body

It may seem as if I have used different words to express the same concept when I use the terms 'body' and 'mind'. There has been a traditional distinction made between the body and the psyche, even though the concept itself represents a unity. In speaking about traditional concepts, I have used body and mind. When speaking about deeper contexts, for example the individual character structure, I have used body and, on occasion, soul (as the supposed opposite) because this better describes the state of suffering in the split personality, where self-alienated activity dominates the structure. The healthy person is the mind/body — in integrity — the 'thinking body'.

Hypotonic muscles

Hypotony refers to varying degrees of flaccidity in under-developed muscles. The respiratory response is negligible, but here lies a potential resource. This is described as 'anticipatory content'.

When the potential resource is reawakened by the therapist's hand, the respiratory response is involuntary — a signal of possibility which announces that the 'thinking body' is now ready for further progress toward total awakening. In the awakened, 'alive' being, respiratory response will be integrated into the breathing wave.

Musculature

By the term musculature, I mean the essential part of man that allows him movement in both emotional and motor spheres. The musculature is the gateway for evaluating patient resources and is a tool that assists the therapeutic process. It is the medium for the integration of mind/body.

Hypertonic muscles

Hypertony refers to varying degrees of tenseness in the musculature. The muscles are weighted down by respiration which is deliberate, conscious, forced. A tense muscle may seem to the inexperienced hand to contain 'energy'. What is being felt are the vibrations of a taut cord, the forced panting for air of a muscle under stress.

Growth centre

Objectively, it is seen as the sum of the body growth areas in a topological sense. Subjectively, it is experienced as the body area (or the sum of body areas) under formation in the existential sense. Growth centres in the process of integration assert themselves as newly won modes of expression.

Growth element

A dimension whose mission is to mass modes of expression by moving in and out of the growth centre, depositing new tasks, which the growth centre in turn incorporates and uses in further growth and adaptation.

Integration

When challenges for new dimensions are incorporated into oneself, then the way for integration — the ultimate goal — occurs as a matter of course. On this basis, the sudden stillness at the end of the struggle in growth is the point of integration. All other experience is a striving towards this event.

Nuclear phenomenon

Point of origin for all emanations of impulse and expression continuing through all developmental stages. At critical phases, frustration of the integration process is experienced by the nuclear phenomenon. It is influenced by the philosophical attitude toward life or death. ·

Anticipatory content

The hidden, unexperienced content is so vivid that the respiration seems to be 'knocking at the door', objectively touched and heard as a vivid and unique impression of pulsing wave in the musculature in question. It is content inhibited in early childhood; when reawakened the incomprehensible is made comprehensible in the child's world.

Resources/Resource-oriented

Resources have their basis in how far spontaneous respiration is incorporated in the breathing during different steps in development. The concept was first used by me in this context in 1963 in order to signify the focussing on latent forces in

Integrated Respiration Theory. I sometimes refer to resources as anticipatory content.

Balance

This is the point of being as equally full of the atmosphere as of oneself.

Muscle quality

Muscle quality is the living phenomenon which gives the musculature its character of tangible life. Muscle quality indicates the richness, the nuances of expressive possibility. The division between consistency and quality is of course an abstraction in contrast to the palpable whole, but essential in passing along and crystallizing experience. Somewhat over-simplified, one can say that consistency covers the material aspect of musculature, and quality refers to 'being' (assessment).

Muscle consistency

A concept defined in relation to what the hand searches for, and as the immediate impression felt by the fingertips during examination. It is a foundation of measurement in relation to the ideal, an optimal functioning in 'consistence to nature', which is only recognized by constant searching and training.

REFERENCES

Johnsen L 1964 Nye synspunkter i psycho-fysioterapeutisk kombinasjonsbehandling. Nordisk psykologi 4
Johnsen L 1966 Indikasjoner og prognose ved muskelterapi. Universitetsforlaget, Oslo
Johnsen L 1970 Integrated respiration therapy. Sem og Stenersen, Oslo.
Johnsen L 1973 Muscular tonus and integrated respiration. Energy and Character: 3
Johnsen L 1975 IRT — Integrert respirasjonsterapi/teori åndedrettsrespirasjon kropp-psyke. Universitetsforlaget, Oslo
Johnsen L 1976 En nøgle til livsgledens skjulte kilde — IRT. Borgen Forlag, København
Johnsen L 1981 IRT, birth and rebirth in the fullness of time. Tullsa Psychiatric Foundation Inc.

Reich W 1949 Character analysis. Orgone Institute Press, New York

For 40 years I have worked and studied in the field of psychotherapy. My theory and therapy have developed in close collaboration with my patients. None of the existing literature has been of specific importance in this development, mainly because literature would have distracted me. My therapy and theory have emerged from the heart of patients. Symbolically speaking, this is the tree of life and not the tree of knowledge.

This is the reason why I have not included a list of references with different authors.

Annotated bibliography

AUTOGENIC TRAINING

Bailey R D 1984 Autogenic training and sickness absence amongst nurses in general training. Journal of Advanced Nursing 9: 581–587
   A longitudinal study using an experimental and control group design was carried out with student nurses using autogenic regulation training. It concluded that autogenic training has a contribution to make in preparing student nurses to cope with the demands of nursing and sickness absence.

Elkins D, Anchor K N, Sandler H M 1978 Physiological effects of relaxation training. American Journal of Clinical Biofeedback 1: 30
   In this experiment EMG readings are used to evaluate the effects of a standardized relaxation training procedure on stress management.

Haley J 1963 Strategies of psychotherapy. Grune and Stratton, New York, pp 201
   The author is an authority on human communication. In the book he deals with the strategies of psychotherapists and patients as they manipulate each other in the process of treatment. The book has valuable information, even for professionals who are not doing psychotherapy.

Hartmann L M 1982 Anxiety, imagery and self-regulation. Journal of Psychiatric Treatment and Evaluation 4(4): 333–336
   The differential effectiveness of two relaxation procedures in an anxiety-reducing programme is examined. The autogenic training procedure is compared with progressive relaxation in people who report high or low vividness of imagery.

Hoppe K D 1961 Relaxation through concentration — concentration through relaxation. Medical Times 89: 254–263
   The author learnt autogenic training from J H Schultz in the 50s. He presents a brief, simple outline of the method and its applicability, sharing clinical experiences.

Janssen K, Neutgens J 1986 Autogenic training and progressive relaxation in the treatment of three kinds of headache. Behaviour Research and Therapy 24(2): 199–208
   The effects of autogenic training and muscular relaxation as self-control procedures are compared in this treatment programme. Headache patients are divided into tension-headache, migraine or combined headache groups.

Roszell D K, Chaney E C 1982 Autogenic training in a drug abuse program. The International Journal of the Addictions 17(8): 1337–1349
   The authors present autogenic training as a useful modality in a drug abuse

treatment programme. Case histories of patients with stress-related problems are described.

Schneider H G et al 1987 Initial relaxation response: contrasts between clinical patients and normal volunteers. Perceptual and Motor Skills 64: 147–153
 In this experiment frontalis EMG and surface skin temperature are used to compare the effectiveness of different relaxation methods using a within-subject design.

Shapiro D H 1982 Overview: clinical and physiological comparison of meditation with other self-control strategies. American Journal of Psychiatry 139: 267–274
 In 1977, the American Psychiatric Association called for a critical examination of the clinical effectiveness of meditation. The author reviews the pertinent literature, and also compares meditation with self-regulation strategies like biofeedback, hypnosis and progressive relaxation.

PSYCHOMOTOR THERAPY

Braatøy T 1947 'De nervøse Sinn.' Cappelen Forlag, Oslo
 'De nervøse Sinn' is a book which gives the reader an insight into the interaction between body and mind through several case histories.
 The therapeutic approach of Braatøy is described in detail and is related to basic psychological knowledge. Braatøy's ability to connect experiences and practical clinical insight to psychology is unique and fascinating. His book is extraordinary also in the way it is written, and reveals a man who has intuition and creativity as well as wide experience in medicine and the social sciences.

Braatøy T 1954 Fundamentals of psychoanalytic technique. John Wiley, New York
 Unlike most other books in the field Braatøy takes as his standpoint the feelings and emotions of the analyst, and in this connection — contrary to the traditional view — gives the student seemingly unlimited freedom in his approaches. From time to time Braatøy permits himself to digress outside psychoanalysis proper, as he feels that every psychoanalytic treatment transcends the limit of proper psychoanalysis.
 Dr Braatøy holds that the problems one encounters in so-called character analysis have not been described or discussed to the extent that they deserve from a practical point of view. His comments on such matters are to some extent contributions to an understanding of W. Reich's character analysis in the same way as his comments on the analyst's emotions and transference problems must be related to Freud's papers on technique.

Bunkan B H 1985 Muskelspenninger og kroppsbilde. Universitetsforlaget, Oslo
 The book is based on the idea of the mind and body as an interacting unit. This is expressed in the way we breathe and move, the state of our muscles, and in the image we have of our body. Treatment is based on the patient's history of disease and a physical examination in which the therapist forms an idea of the patient's body image and potential. A number of physical therapeutic methods are discussed in relation to the patient's resources. The book is addressed to physiotherapists, doctors, psychologists and others whose work is directly concerned with people's health.

Bunkan B H, Thornquist E, Radøy L 1982 Psykomotorisk behandling, Universitetsforlaget, Oslo
 The book contains interviews with the co-founder of psychomotor therapy, Aadel Bülow-Hansen, and with co-workers and patients. It attempts to

describe and analyse the method itself and the changes it brings about in therapists and patients whose emotions and associations are also recorded. The book is primarily written for physiotherapists, psychologists and physicians, but will also be useful for other health workers and for patients.

Christiansen B 1963 Thus speaks the body. (Body movement; perspectives in research). Aruo Press, New York
In the preface the author says: 'It has been written with the aim of bringing together in a fairly systematic way various viewpoints, hypotheses and experimental findings concerning somatic and non-verbal aspects of personality dynamics'. The purpose of the book is to stimulate interest, with the hope of inviting discussions and exchange of opinions'.
The material presented is gathered from the time when the author was a clinical psychologist at an Institute for Child Psychiatry in Oslo. The Nic Waal Institute was a fairly unique place because of its strong emphasis on a monistic psychosomatic approach towards mental illness and health.

Thornquist E 1983 Lungefysioterapi. Universitetsforlaget, Oslo
The aim of this book is to arouse interest in breathing and breathing problems as a whole, including those outside the scope of classical medical diagnoses. Breathing problems are described in the context of posture, movement habits and muscular tension. The book contains descriptions of relevant examination procedures and descriptions and discussions of a broad variety of therapeutic approaches. The author stresses the importance of treating breathing problems indirectly.

Thornquist E, Bunkan H 1986 Hva er psykomotorisk behandling Universitetsforlaget, Oslo
The authors stress the importance of portraying psychomotor therapy both as a concrete therapy and as a framework for understanding.
This form of therapy departs fundamentally from traditional approaches to somatic ailments and is rooted in an understanding of the body which differs from the prevailing one. Local pains and symptoms are viewed as an imbalance in the body as a whole; consequently the entire body is subject to treatment.
The aim of psychomotor therapy is a process of bodily re-orientation based on posture, musculature and respiration. Simultaneously, and inseparable from the bodily process, profound emotional and psychic changes take place.

Psychomotor therapy has been developed from experimental practice. Its founders are T. Braatøy (psychiatrist) and A. Bülow-Hansen (physiotherapist). Relatively little has been recorded in the written form and the psychomotor tradition is mainly passed on through practice.

PHYSIOTHERAPY IN PSYCHIATRIC CARE

Dropsy J 1973 Vivre dans son corps. In Swedish: 1987 Leva i sin kropp Natur & Kultur, Stockholm
Dropsy presents his theoretical and philosophical view and knowledge of man. From many years of practical therapeutic experience and with an unusual combination of theoretical knowledge he describes functions of movement and breathing, based on different holistic views of man. With posture and balance of the body as a starting point, the author describes a person's capacity to express himself and to relate physically and psychologically to his surroundings.

Dropsy J 1984 Le corps bien accordé, Paris. In Swedish: 1988 Den harmoniska kroppen. Natur & Kultur, Stockholm

In this book Dropsy presents movement exercises, their background, performance, effects and limitations. He describes exercises for breathing, sitting, standing, vocalizing and walking.

The movement exercises are mainly built on the theories in *Vivre dans son corps* which have been given a practical application in the form of movement exercises in *Le corps bien accordé*. The exercises are sufficiently simple that after some training they can become part of everyday life as 'invisible' exercises. They are described so thoroughly that it is possible to apply them directly after reading the book.

Goldberg M, 1974 Uber meine Therapieformel in der konzentrativen Bewegungstherapie, Praxis der Psychotherapie no. 6

In her article Goldberg describes an examination of patients' complaints that she uses when giving individual concentrated movement therapy. In interviewing the patient, the author investigates the complaints with regard to the passive or active part of the day, to timing and duration, to the quality of the complaints with a phenomenological description, and to the situation in total. Information from this examination about the variation of the complaints can give the therapist and the patient hints about how to establish suitable individualized future treatment.

May P R A et al 1963 Non-verbal techniques in the re-establishment of body-image and self identity — a preliminary report. Psychiatric Research Report no 16

May et al present theories about body ego and body ego technique which is a treatment method developed by the dance therapists J. Salkin and T. Schoop. In the study reported, chronic schizophrenic patients have been treated with body ego technique. The study was preliminary, but the authors have found that, among other effects, the patients (who were mentally disturbed to a high degree) have become more accessible to verbal therapy through non-verbal treatment.

Roxendal G. 1985 Body awareness therapy and the body awareness scale, treatment and evaluation in psychiatric physiotherapy (thesis), Göteborg (Available from: Roxendal G, Institut för Sjukgymnastik, Lunds universitet, Box 5134, 220 05 Lund)

The treatment method body awareness therapy is based upon a clearly defined holistic view of the patient. The method is described below.

A rating scale, Body Awareness Scale (BAS), based on the principle of the psychiatric rating scale, was constructed and tested with schizophrenic patients. The inter-rater-reliablity score was satisfactory for both psychologists and physiotherapists. A factor analysis was computed, showing factors such as movement, anxiety, body image and general feeling of illness. The factors seem to be of both clinical and scientific interest.

A clinical study was performed with chronic schizophrenic patients. The results of the study showed that the BAS is preliminarily valid and that 6 months of Body Awareness Therapy may decrease anxiety and increase body image and movement functions in schizophrenic patients.

PSYCHOLOGICAL FACTORS IN RECOVERY FROM PHYSICAL DISABILITY

Brewin C R, Shapiro D A 1979 Beliefs about self and their importance for motivation in rehabilitation. In: Osborne D J, Bruneberg M M, Eiser J R (eds) Research in psychology medicine, Vol 2

This is a most useful paper which approaches the problem of motivation in rehabilitation from a psychological perspective. It deals briefly with goal setting and client expectations, and introduces factors which may be related to good coping such as perceived control, helplessness and attributions for culpability; it also makes suggestions about how understanding more about motivation may enable us to help our patients/clients more effectively.

Bryan J F, Locke E A 1967 Goal setting as a means of increasing motivation. Journal of Applied Psychology 51(3): 274–277
    Though this is a small study it illustrates well the effect of specific goal setting as against 'do your best' instructions. Its importance lies in the way in which it highlights the motivating effects of specific goal setting on performance.

Folkman S, Lazarus R S 1980 An analysis of coping in a middle-aged community sample. Journal of Health and Social Behaviour 21: 219–239
    The main strength of this study is that it is about actual coping in a real life situation. This is in contrast to many other studies where people are asked how they would cope in various stressful situations.

Ley P 1982 Giving information to patients. In: Eiser J M (ed) Social psychology and behaviourial science. Wiley, London
    This chapter addresses seven key questions on giving information to patients and provides a review of work in relation to each question. A useful and very comprehensive list of references is also given.

Lipowski Z J 1970 Physical illness, the individual and the coping process. Psychiatry in Medicine 1: 91–102
    Though an early reference, it is useful as it deals specifically with physical illness. It also provides a clear introduction to the concepts of coping style and coping strategies.

Visotsky H N, Hamburg D A, Goss M E, Lebovits B V 1961 Coping behaviour under extreme stress, observations of patients with severe poliomyelitis. Archives of General Psychiatry 5: 423–448
    Another early reference, but a classical descriptive study of patients with extremely severe and life threatening illness, which is based on careful observation. It provides insights into the way individuals cope and highlights the number of different factors which may affect coping.

Wallston K A, Wallston B S, Smith S, Dobbins C J 1987 Perceived control and health. Current Psychological Research and Review 6.1: 525
    An excellent article which explores beliefs about perceived control and their relationship to health behaviour. An extensive list of over 100 references is provided which covers most recent work of importance in this area.

Partridge C J, Johnston M J A study of patients attending for physiotherapy with physical disability following a stroke and a Colles' fracture. British Journal of Clinical Psychology, in press
    Results showed patients who believed in personal control over their recovery achieved more beneficial outcomes.

REHABILITATION OF TORTURE VICTIMS

Barfoed G, Bjerregaard B, Busch E et al 1982 Physical therapy of torture victims. Danske Fysioterapeuter (19)
    A report on the experience of treating 30 victims with physical therapy over the course of two years. Working principles and methods of treatment

are described. Physical therapy is an important link in the rehabilitation of torture victims.

Cohn J, Danielsen L, Mygind Holzer, K I et al 1985 A study of Chilian refugee children in Denmark. Lancet, Aug. 24: 437–438
     The study concerns 85 Chilian children whose parents have been tortured — the psychological as well as social sequelae from which the children suffer.

Genefke I K, Marcussen H, Sørensen B 1987 Rehabilitation of torture victims: teaching. In: Health hazards of organised violence. Proceedings of a working group on health hazards of organised violence. Veldhoven Apr. 22–25, 1986 Hague: Ministry of Welfare, Health and Cultural Affairs, pp 155–163
     The paper describes RCT's teaching and information activities and the great impact these have had. RCT considers that it has a duty to spread the message that torture victims need assistance and can be helped back to a decent and dignified existence, to health staff not only in Denmark but in the whole world.

Lunde I 1982 Mental sequelae to torture. Månedsskrift for praktisk lægegerning: Aug
     The author describes the mental sequelae found in 135 torture victims examined by the Danish Medical Group 1975–79 and the method that was used, and compares the mental sequelae with the stress symptom complexes known as the concentration camp syndrome and the war sailor syndrome. The author stresses the need for a special institution with experts in various fields for the rehabilitation of torture victims.

Lunde I, Boysen G, Ortmann J 1987 Rehabilitation of torture victims: treatment and research. In: Health hazards of organised violence. Proceedings of a working group on health hazards of organised violence. Veldhoven Apr. 22–25 1986. Hague: Ministry of Welfare, Health and Cultural Affairs, pp 136–148
     The paper describes the development of the treatment model and the activities of RCT so far. It also describes the research and the background for the choice of research methods at RCT. Because today there is not sufficient knowledge concerning treatment methods and their effects in respect of torture victims, RCT have just commenced a prospective study to examine the effects of treatment.

Rasmussen O V, Marcussen H 1982 The somatic sequelae to torture. Månedsskrift for praktisk lægegerning, March
     Amnesty International's medical group has examined about 500 torture victims from Greece, Spain, Chile, Argentina and Northern Ireland and the results from the first 135 Danish examinations have been analysed. The form of torture involved various types of physical and mental violence. The investigation revealed a complex picture of sequelae involving most body systems.

Somnier F, Genefke I K 1986 Psychotherapy for victims of torture. British Journal of Psychiatry 149: 232–329
     Three groups of torture victims were studied with the aim of establishing a concept of psychotherapy for such victims. The results of this study formed the basis for the course.

Svendsen G 1985 When dealing with torture victims, social work involves the entire family. Socialrådgiveren 11
     The paper describes the role of the social worker and the purpose of social work at the RCT, Copenhagen, and gives a case history as an example of the help a victim received.

Tornberg A, Jacobsen L 1985 & 1986 Violation of human rights and the nursing profession. In: International Nursing Review 32(6): 178–180; 33(1): 6–8
   The first paper describes violation of human rights and the nurses' responsibility in respecting human rights. In the second paper the focus is on torture and its after effects on the individual and the responsibility of the nursing profession in this tragic context. There is description of the principles of nursing torture victims.

International Rehabilitation and Research Center for Torture Victims 1985 Annual Report 1984

PSYCHOLOGICAL FACTORS IN THE PHYSICAL REHABILITATION OF TORTURE

Janoff-Bulman R 1985 The aftermath of victimization: Rebuilding shattered assumptions. In: Figley C R (ed) Trauma and its wake. Brunner/Mazel, New York
   A section in *Trauma and It's Wake: The Study and Treatment of Post-Traumatic Stress Disorder* which focusses on the nature of the trauma itself, diagnosis of PTSD and its treatment.

Tymieniecka A T 1962 Phenomenology and science in contemporary European thought. Polish Institute of Arts and Sciences, Poland
   A discussion of existential psychology and phenomenology with a focus on the development of the 'lived world' of the individual.

Lazarus R C 1977 Cognitive and coping processes in emotion. In: Monat A, Lazarus R (eds) Stress and coping. Columbia University Press, New York
   A compendium of articles on cognitive psychology, theories of stress, and characteristics of effective coping behaviour.

Piaget J 1971 Biology and knowledge. University of Chicago Press, Chicago
   A basic discussion of the principles of his theory on cognitive development, epistemology and developmental psychology.

Fishman W A 1978 Organic psychiatry. Blackwell Scientific Publications, New York
   A review of the major categories of organic brain dysfunction and implications for diagnosis and treatment of neuropsychiatric problems which result.

Lezak M D 1983 Neuropsychological assessment, 2nd edn. Oxford University Press, New York
   A review of the basis for the practice of clinical neuropsychology including rationales for protocols for neuropsychological assessment and patient treatment.

Watzlawik P, Beavin J, Jackson D 1967 Pragmatics of human communications. W W Norton, Inc, New York
   A presentation of neuro/psycholinquistics as a basis for understanding human communication.

INTEGRATED RESPIRATION THERAPY

Johnsen L 1950 Muscular-Respiratory Diagnosis Scheme
   The coloured figures — a symbolic colour language, on which I have based the IRT developmental theory.

Johnsen L 1964 Nye synspunkter i psyko-fysioterapeutisk kombinasjonsbehandling. Nordisk Psykologi
   The article shows the author's concepts regarding underdeveloped muscular-respiratory conditions, e.g. shifting of therapeutic approach away from traditional thinking based on tensions and defence.

Johnsen L 1966 Indikasjoner og prognose ved muskelterapi. Universitetsforlaget, Oslo
   The book presents two cases which show how the colours used when charting patients may change as a result of the reintegrating process.

Johnsen L 1970 Integrated respiration therapy. Sem og Stenersen, Oslo
   The purpose of the book is to demonstrate a child therapy in which drawings and dreams are integrated parts of the process.

Johnsen L 1975 Birth and rebirth in the fullness of time. The breathing me. Universitetsforlaget, Oslo
   The book demonstrates the developmental theory, the healthy growth of the child from birth to puberty. The different steps of development are described by the patients' own experiences when they progressively reestablish their own autonomy.

Index

Abuse victims
  case study, 148–149
  existential aspects, 146–147,
    151–152
  integration of psychological factors, 11,
    145–152
  neuropsychological sequelae,
    149–151
  psychic consequences, 147–149
  see also Torture victims
Achievement motivation, 105–106
  see also Goals and goal-setting;
    Motivation
Adaptive response, 108, 109–112
Adherence, 112–115
Affiliation, 106
Alexander technique, 95
Amnesty International, 121–122
Anticipatory content, 163, 180, 184,
    185
Anxiety
  in autogenic training, 26, 31, 32,
    33–34, 35–36
  see also Torture victims
Apperception tests, 105
Appraisal, disability and, 109–112
Art of movement, Laban, 96
Aspiration, recovery and, 106–107
Autogenic training, 12, 19–43, 94
  bibliography, 191–192
  case studies, 31–32, 33–36, 37–39
  challenges of, 39–40
  goals and goal-setting, 29–30
  group therapy, 23–24
  ideomotoric training and, 22–23
  relaxation dosage, 24–25, 34
  relevance, 19–20
  selection of patients, 26–28
    general indications, 26–27
    physiotherapeutic evaluation,
      27–28
  theoretical considerations, 20–25

application, 22–25
method, 20–22
professional cooperation, 25
psychological mechanisms, 23
training of therapists, 40–42
treatment contract, 28–30
treatment process, 30–39
  evaluation phase, 31–32
  final phase, 36–39
  initial phase, 32–35
  mid-phase, 35–36
Autohypnosis, *see* Autogenic training
Autonomic function, 59, 61, 95
Awareness Through Movement, 96

Balance/equilibrium
  in IRT, 166–168, 186
  in psychomotor therapy, 52–54, 57,
    61, 69
Behaviour modification programmes,
    114
Bibliography
  autogenic training, 191–192
  Integrated Respiration Therapy, 197
  physiotherapy in psychiatric care,
    193–194
  psychological factors in recovery
    from physical disability,
    194–195
  psychomotor therapy, 192–193
  rehabilitation of torture victims,
    142–143, 195–197
Birth, IRT and, 160–164
  rebirth experience, 161–162
Body awareness
  abuse victims and, 151
  autogenic training and, 34–35, 37,
    38, 39, 41, 42
  psychomotor therapy and, 59–60,
    67–68
  torture victims and, 127, 130, 140,
    151